REAP THE BENEFITS OF
OPERATIONAL EXCELLENCE

Proven Principles and Methodologies to Achieve Increased Profitability

Reap the Benefits of Operational Excellence
Proven Principles and Methodologies to Achieve Increased Profitability

Copyright ©2016 by S. Michael Sutherland
All rights reserved. Per the International Copyright Law, the scanning, uploading, and electronic sharing of any part of this book without the permission of the author is unlawful piracy and theft of the author's intellectual property. If you would like to use material from this book, you must obtain prior written permission by contacting the author at smichaelsutherland@gmail.com.
Thank you for supporting the author's rights.

Scripture quotations are taken from the *King James Version* of the Holy Bible.

Quotations marked [Goldratt] are from the book *The Goal: A Process of Ongoing Improvement* by Dr. Eliyahu M. Goldratt and Jeff Cox, Copyright © 1984, 1986, 1992, 2004 by The North River Press Publishing Company. All rights reserved.
ISBN 13: 978-1537513744
ISBN-10: 1537513745

Contents

Acknowledgements

Introduction 5

Chapter 1: First Things, First 9

Chapter 2: Recognize the Important Things 15

Chapter 3: It All Begins with a Sales Agreement 22

Chapter 4: The Organization 29

Chapter 5: Establish Clear, Realistic, and Attainable Goals 40

Chapter 6: The Theory of Constraints 44

Chapter 7: Financial Measurements 47

Chapter 8: Organizational Balance Using Even Flow Principles 52

Chapter 9: The Business Plan: "Plan the Attack Then Attack the Plan" 65

Chapter 10: Process Engineering and Mapping 70

Chapter 11: Constraints 76

Chapter 12: Schedule(s) 83

Chapter 13: Product Development and Purchasing.... 103

Chapter 14: Variances 136

Chapter 15: Produce EXCELLENT Products and Services 143

Chapter 16: Ongoing Improvement, Never Give Up ... 149

Acknowledgements

First, thanks are due to God our Father and to the Lord Jesus Christ. Without the knowledge and abilities that He has given me; this book would not have been possible. God has shown me His faithfulness and favor throughout my life. He has provided me with many opportunities to learn and then apply the principles outlined in this book.

A special thanks to my wife, Elizabeth. She is my best friend and has provided me with unwavering support throughout the years. I am blessed to have her as my partner and extremely thankful to have her in my life. I adore her. She has been primarily responsible for raising our four fantastic children. They, along with their spouses, have become outstanding adults. I am incredibly grateful and honored to be their father. I love them all dearly.

Also, thank you for taking the time to read and study this book.

Introduction

This book is not intended to provide you with specific answers on how to achieve operational excellence, but rather to offer real-life examples of how these principles and methodologies have been successfully applied to positively impact the financial and operational aspects of several companies producing hundreds of millions of dollars in annual revenue. With the information contained in this book, you can take these principles and apply them to virtually any organization or project, regardless of the function or size.

This book is also intended to enhance your thinking about how to best utilize these principles and methodologies within your own company or organization. I prefer to learn by asking questions. Questions can sometimes cause controversy, but questions can also identify the need for change. The correct question usually leads to the correct answer. The people on your team are the best resources of information to answer questions about the current processes and inner workings of your organization. Do not give the answers, ask the right questions. A question is much better. Questions prompt us to use our brains to think things through and find the correct answer to the question or problem. By asking questions, we will have the opportunity to make well-informed decisions. We may find that the answer or part of the answer requires a change, which it usually does. We need to consider how to persuade others to overcome resistance to change. Ask God to give you wisdom. If we follow His covenants and do His will, He has promised to direct our steps. He will provide the insight we need to make the correct decisions and implement the necessary changes at the right time. If we truly listen and do what God says, He will never fail us. It does not matter what position you hold within the organization or what your responsibilities are. You can *reap the Benefits of Operational Excellence* by implementing and utilizing these principles.

Process Improvement is a continual journey, and it takes time, persistence, courage, and a lot of innovative work. We need to crawl before we walk, walk before we run, and run before we sprint. Each step of improvement builds on the others and creates momentum. We always need to give it our best. Nothing worthwhile comes easy. Do not become discouraged. Never give up. There is always a price to pay, but achieving excellence is genuinely remarkable.

We reap what we sow – Sow sparingly, reap sparingly. Sow bountifully, reap bountifully. Therefore, always strive for improvement and honor God. Additionally, maintaining a correct balance in every area of your life is extremely important. Follow God's instructions found in His word.

This book contains numerous examples of disciplines and ideas that have been implemented and successfully utilized to significantly enhance the operations and profitability of production homebuilding companies. These principles and ideas can be used in almost any type of business. You need to consider ways to integrate them into your system and workflow process. I will point out some of the actual benefits we received and what can be accomplished by utilizing the information contained in each chapter. I have tried to keep this book simple. I am sure that if you think creatively about how to use this information, you can achieve many more outstanding benefits.

In the summer of 2011, I was diagnosed with ALS (Lou Gehrig's disease). The ALS has slurred my speech, which leads me to write this book. I know that God has given me an immense amount of valuable experience and information about business operations that I need to share with others. I must tell you that I have had many successes throughout my life, and I have also made mistakes. However, I do know that God is faithful and utterly true to all His word. He loves us all beyond what we can imagine, and He is a wonderful, caring God. In times of success and times of difficulty, He has always been there. He tells us that He will never leave us or forsake us, and I have found that to be true over and over again. I know that He has a good plan for my life, and I am learning to trust in Him completely. I have learned that because I am His, and when I follow His word, He is directing my steps. Everything that happens to me passes through God's hands first. I am not saying that sickness and disease come from God; it does not. I am saying that when I made Christ the Lord of my life, He watches over me and only allows what is best for me, and what teaches me to become more like Him. He has blessed me beyond compare, and He continues to bless Elizabeth and me.

I hope that you are blessed by reading this book and that you benefit from it.

Chapter 1

First Things, First

Why did you start your company, or why do you go to work each day? I am sure you can visualize many good reasons if you give it some thought. But the *primary* goal of any organization, company, or person, if you think about it, is to MAKE MONEY. I used to struggle with that statement or belief. I used to think that being too greedy or self-serving meant focusing too much on making money. However, if you think about it, maximizing profits or making money is truly always the primary goal. "Everything else you do in business is a means to achieve that goal." [Goldratt, 2004] There should be only one main goal of every organization, which is to make money. Making money is a God-ordained endeavor, so we should never feel ashamed of focusing our objectives on earning a living. *GOD IS AN OVERFLOW GOD.* He wants us to prosper. I am not saying that making money is more important than God. It all comes from Him anyway. Our relationship with God should always be in first place in our lives. Everything in life should be in balance. I will discuss balance further in a later chapter.

Every goal or objective should impact positive profit growth. Additionally, every goal or objective should contribute to increasing sales. I am referring to closed or delivered sales. Once the entire process is completed, the product is not truly sold until it is entirely produced, delivered, and the total revenue from the sale is received. I am not referring to just a sales agreement or a cash deposit at the early stages of the process.

I am sure your company or organization has many extremely positive and worthwhile objectives and achievements. However, if your organization is not profitable, all of the good things it does will eventually come to an end, and a different, more profitable organization will carry out those good things. Communicate the goal of making money to your entire organization. Include your internal and external team members. Let them all know your objectives and explain why they should focus on the primary goal of increasing profitability. Include your trade partners, suppliers, and consultants in communicating your goal. Explain to them that your organization's process improvement initiatives will not only save them money but also enhance their operations. This all sounds elementary, but achieving and maintaining profitability improvements requires consistency and perseverance.

Along with profitability, there is another measurement that is critical to the success of any organization. It is called *Cash Flow*. Cash flow is the lifeblood of any business organization. Cash flow is equally as vital as sales to your organization. If you cannot achieve a completed sale because you lack the necessary cash flow to produce the product or service, you are in a difficult position. Cash flow projections and the consistent monitoring of their achievement are crucial to the organization's ongoing success.

Use methods that accurately track your improvement to measure your success. One example of this is productivity. *PRODUCTIVITY* = Accomplishing something in terms of making money. "Productivity brings the company closer to its goal of making money." [Goldratt, 2004] This is just one example. There are many others. You must determine the best measurements for your organization. *Remember, you must manage the capacity of your processes or system to generate revenue.* We will delve into more details about this throughout this book. If you achieve positive results in these areas, you are laying a solid foundation to reap the benefits of operational excellence.

1.1 Why Operational Excellence?

Achieving operational excellence offers numerous potential benefits. One significant outcome of operational excellence will be the ability to increase overall profit margins while adjusting product prices to remain competitive. Allowing for domination of the competition with faster delivery time and setting the pricing by what the market dictates, not the competition. It will encourage the team to continue striving for ongoing improvement and maintain their high morale. Obtaining operational excellence is not an easy task. So why do we strive to receive it and put so much effort into achieving it? Many organizations recognize the need for excellent operations. Still, few are willing to continue the journey when they perceive the required changes and improvements as too challenging and difficult to achieve. Those who give up do not understand how much money they are leaving on the table and all the other benefits they are passing up. As you have heard before, anything worth having does not come easily. It takes knowledge, consistency, courage, and an unwavering will to be the best. Operational excellence **CAN BE** achieved. The principles, methodologies, and ideas discussed in this book have been proven effective. If you and your team utilize the information contained in this book, you **can and you will achieve** operational excellence.

I equate the words "excellence" with "perfection." We are told in God's word to be perfect. But the only perfect human being is Jesus Christ, and he is the Son of God. Jesus tells us in God's word to "be perfect as my Father in heaven is perfect." So, if Jesus tells us to be perfect, it must be attainable. We should always be striving for perfection through the strength that Jesus gives us. God's word also says that "we can do all things through Christ who gives us strength." With Jesus Christ's help, we **CAN DO ALL THINGS**.

I like to describe the word *EXCELLENCE* as a mindset. We strive for perfection, but excellence is a way of life. It requires a mindset that when we try our best and we fall short of perfection, we do not give up. We learn from our experiences, make the necessary changes, and try again. We may have to make a few significant changes or maybe just minor tweaks, but we never give up. That is an excellent mindset. We continue to try, move forward, and improve.

I have consistently found that to achieve excellent operations, one must make changes. Maybe your organization is already operationally strong and very few changes are needed. I believe in the saying that there is always room for improvement. Perhaps after reading this book, you will realize that your organization can be significantly improved operationally, and numerous changes are necessary. Whatever changes your organization needs to make, it is essential to understand that achieving operational excellence will not always be easy, and mistakes will be made along the way.

So, if we say perfection equals excellence. Then, one way to say that excellence equals efficiency. Efficient operations mean excellent operations. I will describe how to achieve operational excellence by creating efficient processes, systems, and enhancing business velocity through the combination of Six Sigma, Lean concepts, and the Theory of Constraints. These are the three most powerful disciplines in continuous improvement. To achieve breakthrough performance, you must align these principles within your organization.

Proven Principles and Methodologies to Achieve Increased Profitability

These principles and methodologies can lead to operational excellence, increased profitability, and numerous remarkable benefits for the organization. The information contained in this book is simple. Do not try to overanalyze the information. Use your common sense to apply these disciplines to the organization. Just remember, Mark Twain once said, "Common sense is not common at all."

Chapter 2

Recognize the Important Things

Mentors in our lives are a gift from God. Each one of us possesses all of the knowledge and abilities we need to achieve His plan for our lives. It all comes from God, but He also uses other people to educate, train, and influence us. Every one of us must give the credit first to God, and then to others that God has brought across our path. Everything that we have learned in life comes from watching others, being taught, reading and studying, experiences, or experimenting with ideas that God has given us. God says He has a plan for each one of us. "He has a good plan, a plan to prosper us, and give us a hope, and a future".

There is power and greater knowledge in having more than just one person involved in decision-making. God says that "Where two or more of you are gathered, there He is also". Yes, you may have the responsibility of making the final decision, but having counsel or information from God and others is extremely valuable. I have found that having feedback and information from a diverse group of people is always very helpful in making a decision. I am not saying that you should try to please everyone with your decision, but collecting diverse opinions and information are beneficial in making your final decision.

What I am saying is that the credit should go to many very talented individuals who have worked with me and taught me the information contained in this book, as well as much more.

I want to mention George Casey, the CEO of Zaring Homes at the time, for introducing me to the writings of Dr. Goldratt. My first exposure to "The Theory of Constraints" (T.O.C.) [Goldratt, 1984] was during my time with Zaring Homes. *Quality Time Management* was a part of the Zaring Homes business model, which included building new homes in sixty calendar days. Without learning and implementing the T.O.C., this would not have been possible. George took me under his wing and taught me how the principles of T.O.C. work in production homebuilding. The book "The Goal" by Dr. Eliyahu M. Goldratt has had a profound influence on my career. My knowledge and application of "The Theory of Constraints" [Goldratt, 1984] have aided me immensely in achieving success throughout my career. I had the opportunity to meet and have lunch with Dr. Goldratt before his death. That lunch meeting provided me with a deeper understanding of the principles underlying his teaching, and I have endeavored to share some of them in this book, along with real-life examples of how these principles and methodologies were applied. I would highly recommend all of Dr. Goldratt's writings.

Additionally, I would like to thank Scott Chaikin. He taught me to be an assertive leader and to have the commitment to always strive to be the best at what I do. Some of the quotes used in this book came directly from him.

I want to extend special thanks to the former owners of Village Homes of Colorado. They trusted me and allowed me the opportunity to implement these principles and the needed operational changes. Many of the actual examples used in this book were done during my years with Village Homes.

We should not be reluctant to give credit to others. If we have learned from, received good counsel, or gained insights from others, we should provide them with credit. A key aspect of building trust and loyalty as a leader is to give credit when it is due.

Your spouse is a great person to get counsel from. God has made you one flesh, so it is like getting a different perspective from yourself. Your spouse has *skin in the game.* They want you to succeed, and you will benefit immensely from their thoughts, ideas, and perspective. Another beneficial group to get counsel from is your trade partners and consultants. They also want to see you and your organization succeed because if your business improves, grows, and becomes more profitable, they know that their companies will do the same. Next, you may consider a type of *Board of Directors*. This group of counselors should encompass a range of proven, successful, and positive business professionals. You need a team of advisors. You should not try to make big decisions in isolation. Several sharp minds working on a solution to a problem are much better than one. We should always surround ourselves with people who are positive, successful, have a desire to be excellent, and a will to win. Please do not listen to those who tell you it cannot be done. God has already equipped us with everything we need to excel and reach our destiny. You need to work to find it within yourself. God says, "faith without works is dead." Keep working to improve and become excellent.

I want to thank many people for teaching me, supporting me, having faith in me, and providing me with the opportunities to implement the disciplines, methods, and ideas discussed in this book. I want to mention them all by name, but there have been so many wonderful and talented people who have positively impacted my life. I have truly benefited in both my personal and professional life. Thanks to all of you.

2.1 Personal Balance

Personal balance is such an important topic that it needs attention early in this book. Personal balance is the valid key to success. We must always maintain a balance between our spiritual, personal, and professional lives. This is the area where I have seen so many people struggle. Throughout my career, I have also struggled to maintain a personal balance.

What is important to you? What means the most to you is where you will spend the majority of your time. Is spending quality time with God important? Is spending quality time with your spouse and family essential? Is spending productive time at work important? Is your leisure time and time for yourself essential? The answer should be *yes* to all of these questions. This book is mainly focused on how to gain the benefits of excellent business operations, but if your life is out of balance in these areas, you are headed for trouble. It will be a long, arduous journey to achieving lasting success. Ask God to help you maintain balance in your life.

We have been taught that to be successful, one must work long and hard. As I pointed out earlier, nothing worthwhile comes easily. There is a price to pay. Is your relationship and fellowship with God worthwhile? Is a loving and stable family worthwhile? Is your job or career rewarding and valuable? We have been led to believe that our job, career, or professional life is most important. I strongly disagree. I do agree that it is essential, but not at the expense of the other worthwhile aspects of your life. God said, "The last would be first and the first would be last". Too many people prioritize collecting "things" over what truly matters in their lives. Each one of us came into this world without "things" and we will leave this world without "things".

We need to seriously consider where our priorities lie. Balance in your life is critical.

My late father used to say, "Take care of the business first and the business will take care of you." I partially agree with him. I disagree that the business needs to always come first before everything else. I know that in the homebuilding business, you could work around the clock. There is always something that needs attention. I am sure most businesses are similar. You must maintain balance in your life. If your professional life outweighs the other worthwhile areas of your life, you are going to suffer. Perhaps even lose a relationship that you realize, too late, was worth fighting for. Our relationships with God and our families also need to be nurtured and cultivated. Yes, our business or job is essential and should never be neglected, but we must maintain a balance in our lives; otherwise, we may lose focus or even sacrifice the things that are most important in life. Having nice things is not bad. God wants to bless his children with nice things, and having nice things is another benefit of obtaining operational excellence. But, do not make acquiring nice things the main objective of life.

We must learn how to work smarter and more efficiently. Another benefit is that we will not have to work longer. Hard work does pay off, but we need to maximize our efforts and resources by implementing innovative, efficient processes. I like the analogy of using an axe. To achieve the desired outcome, we should not try harder, but rather sharpen the blade. Brilliant work equals hard work.

Do you work long hours because you think you have to or because you want to? Either way, if you diligently implement the principles covered in this book, you will produce such outstanding and productive results that you will only have to work regular business hours, creating opportunity for balance in your life. You will not feel the need to be the first in the office each morning and the last to leave each day to impress anyone. You will not be considered a marginal employee; you will be regarded as an exceptional and valued employee. If you are a business owner, do not try to do everything on your own. Run the business; do not let the business run you. Then you can strive for a balance in your life.

All that you have are God's love and the love of your family. Please always remember they don't need all of your time, but they want and deserve some of it. Give them the love and the quality time they want and need. Make it a priority to maintain balance in all worthwhile areas of your life.

Chapter 3

It All Begins with a Sales Agreement

Sales are the foundation of any business organization. Everything starts with a Sales Agreement or some contract to purchase the product or service offered. If there is no market demand for the product or service, there is no need for operations at all. There must be sales that are profitable, improving, and growing, especially in a startup organization. The organization may not be financially stable from the outset due to initial costs, loans, and other expenses. Still, the profit margin from selling the product or service should be sufficient to generate a profit from the beginning.

To maintain a healthy organization, a good balance between sales operations and production operations is essential. If there is more emphasis on one over the other, the organization will never be as profitable as it could and should be. If there is a profitable sale, but the organization lacks adequate operations to complete the product efficiently and effectively, the expected profit will be eroded or possibly lost entirely. The organization should be treated as a team—each function should work productively together to achieve extraordinary success.

I, like most entrepreneurs, know and understand the importance of achieving *speed to market* with sales. I agree with the entrepreneur's thoughts that getting the product to market quickly to generate sales revenue and cash flow is critical. Yes, securing a customer sale or contract upfront is extremely valuable. Hopefully, doing so will remove the customer from the market. Still, a sale is not truly complete until the completed product is delivered to the customer and all revenue from the sale has been collected and deposited into your bank account.

Communicating the proper expectations to the customer is essential from the beginning. Customers must fully understand the sales process requirements and the benefits that sales operations bring to them. The Sales Agreement in homebuilding, as an example, should contain items such as:

- The home to be sold (built), Plan name or number, elevation designation, and garage orientation.
- The Legal Description of the property.
- Purchase price of the home and site.
- Deposits.
- Payment terms.
- Selections, Options, and Upgrades.
- Special Requests and Change Orders.
- Time is of the essence.
- Amendments and Attachments.
- Start and completion of construction.

- Required orientations and site visits.
- Construction Schedule.
- House plan and material changes.
- Model Homes, marketing materials, and brochures.
- Customer alterations are not allowed.
- Insurance obligations.
- Neighborhood and site conditions.
- Homeowners' Association.
- Redundancy Code.
- Warranties.
- Mold and radon gas disclaimer.
- Breach of agreement and remedies.
- Miscellaneous.
- Liability.
- Entire agreement.
- Receipt and Review of Documents. (List all Documents)
- Authority to sign the Agreement.

This list serves as a guideline, and additional categories and details may be required under each line item. The key point is that the majority of the work needs to be completed before the product is produced. I have learned through the years that a large percentage of the work needs to be completed upfront by setting proper expectations, having complete and accurate documentation, agreements, and processes that deal with everyone associated with the organization, especially the customer.

Capture as many sales contracts as the current system can produce. Create a manageable backlog of product orders to maintain a steady production flow. However, the number of actual completed and closed products should determine market demand or the start pace, not just a sales contract upfront. You set your market demand by the current amount of throughput your system can produce. If you can currently increase throughput (sales), or if you have to decrease throughput to meet market conditions or demand, then do so. Please note that there may be seasonal fluctuations in sales orders, so be prepared to adjust the system accordingly. The market is constantly changing. Producing a product without selling it increases costly inventory and operational expenses. An example in homebuilding of expensive, not sold inventory is Speculation Homes or Move-in Ready homes. You must balance production flow with market demand while always maintaining even flow principles. I will discuss *Even Flow* in more detail later.

Figure out what it takes to be competitive in the market based on the current processes of the organization. Conduct extensive *Market Research*. Thoroughly understand the market and its competition. Research the product or service the competitor is providing in detail. Know their marketing, sales strategy, and pricing structure. Learn everything about them so the advantage is maintained. Promote your organization and the products and services it provides. Always continue market research. Look for emerging technologies or changing market trends that make once-strong processes obsolete.

Every operational improvement builds upon itself and produces a higher level of profitability. If you respond to the market faster, you gain an advantage in the marketplace. With operational excellence, you could virtually deliver your product in half the time. That means more customers, more revenue, and more net profit. Once the operational improvements are in place, go to the marketplace and advertise quicker delivery of your product.

Additionally, another significant advantage of operational excellence is the ability to offer what I call *Crafted Customization in a Production Environment.* The organization can offer the customer full customization of the product at production pricing. By doing so, the organization can market this as a significant selling point over its competitors. Ideally, operationally speaking, all the limited options that are offered on a product would be chosen before production begins. Similar to the process of ordering a new car, all the desired options available on a product are selected at the dealership before the order is sent to the manufacturing plant, with no changes allowed once production of the new car begins. However, we have further enhanced the process to differentiate ourselves from our competitors. After the organizations' processes had been fine-tuned, we instituted what was termed the *Special Requests* process. In this process, the customer was allowed to request the design and pricing of virtually any feasible customization of the product, regardless of whether it was an enhancement to a standard option or a newly created design. A part of the Special Request process required the customer to pay an upfront nonrefundable fee of $250.00 for each request to cover the costs of design and pricing. If the customer ultimately chose to purchase the customization, the fee would be credited toward the price of the new option. The sales, design, and pricing process that had been implemented and refined allowed customers to quickly select from standard options and special requests. Certain team members were assigned to address incoming special requests as a priority. The sales process required the customer to make all option selections and special requests before the product was slotted for production to assure there were no delays once production began. However, another benefit was that the customer was allowed to make selection changes and additional special requests after production had begun, provided they were made within specific *Cutoff Dates*. The cutoff dates were defined to ensure that the proposed changes or additional items would not adversely impact the schedule or lead times, and would provide adequate time for the updated information to be disseminated to the relevant individuals. If the customer made the requested change on or before the cutoff date, the change would be allowed. Requested changes to items that were specified as part of a previous cutoff

The requested change would not be allowed. There MUST BE NO EXCEPTIONS to this process.

Another benefit that can be derived from operational excellence is to charge a *Premium* for specifying a product delivery date. Many customers are willing to pay extra money for a guaranteed delivery time. I will discuss how to achieve this throughout this book.

Many organizations focus the majority of their efforts on increasing sales and revenue from year to year. Increased sales and revenue may keep executive management and the shareholders satisfied. Still, they do not realize how much additional profit and other benefits can be achieved by improving overall operations. Sales and efficient sales operations are critical, but not at the expense of other functional operations. Significant sales operations without solid production operations leave potential extra revenue and profits on the table, not to mention dissatisfied customers. There must be a good balance in everything.

A necessary process that continues throughout the entire workflow system deals with *Customer Relationship Management* (CRM). Frequent *touchpoints with the customer keep* them engaged and positive about the whole experience with the organization. The CRM process should be designed to maintain the customer's excitement about their purchase throughout the delivery process and beyond. This process, if executed with excellence, has a tremendous positive impact on the customer's overall satisfaction. The phrase "The customer always comes first" is most definitely true.

Chapter 4

The Organization

There is a great deal to consider regarding the organization. I have not tried to cover every area, but instead address a few topics that are vital to the success of every organization. We need to focus on having a vigorous, efficient, productive, and healthy organization to achieve ongoing improvement and operational excellence. If the team does not fully understand where you want to lead them and why, if they do not buy into your process of improvement or reorganization, then you are fighting an uphill battle. The resistance to change is already present, and if the team is not behind you or willing to wholeheartedly follow your lead, achieving operational excellence, positive results, and growth will become exceedingly difficult. I will discuss several important areas to address. Still, one of the most critical is to gather information from the team and let them know that their input is instrumental in shaping the direction the organization is taking. Everyone in the organization should hear your plans simultaneously to ensure a consistent message is delivered and received. I have found that *Quarterly Team Meetings* are the best way to accomplish this. At this meeting, the whole team is gathered in the same room at the same time. The meeting lends itself well to conveying the information that is deemed appropriate, allowing everyone to hear it together.

Create a culture of trust throughout the organization. The team needs to know that every individual, regardless of their position, job function, and responsibilities, is essential and valuable. The entire organization is one team, and they must perform as one. Break away from traditional leadership techniques or styles. Be a leader, not a manager. To lead and facilitate the kind of atmosphere that will be needed, your team must trust you. Be honest, open, complete, of integrity, and transparent. Be genuine and sincere. Have a passion for change and ongoing improvement. Your team will recognize your commitment and follow your lead.

Create a culture of *Mutual Admiration*. The team must believe that each member has value. Teach them to admire and respect one another, and to support each other. Every individual and every department of the organization must work together. The entire organization is *One Big Team.* Placing blame or engaging in finger-pointing should not be tolerated in the organization's culture under any circumstances. We all make mistakes, especially when we are making changes and trying new things to improve. Let the team know that errors are not wanted, but lead them and reward them for not hiding or covering up the mistakes. The team members are generally not bad, but the processes may be flawed. Create a safe environment for them to *pull the Cord* and stop the workflow if a mistake or problem is discovered before the defective work is allowed to proceed down the line. I will explain this in more detail later. I have found that a significant portion of your success is attributed to your personality and leadership abilities. Be a leader, not a dictator. Your people must trust you.

Concentrate on the team's positives instead of their negatives. Find a team member doing something correctly or excelling and send them a handwritten personal note of praise and appreciation. Make them feel valued. A person will go above and beyond if they feel valued. Create a culture where the *Open Door Policy* is genuinely open and accessible. Clear, open, and honest communication is vital and key to success and obtaining operational excellence.

Think of every department or function of the organization as a link in the same chain. Remember, a chain is only as strong as its weakest link. I will explain how to make each link strong, efficient, and effective. Additionally, foster a culture of discipline and accountability. Accountability is a good thing. Everyone should be fully aware of their complete scope of work and be disciplined not to let their work move down the line to the next department until it is finished to the expected quality. Each individual should be in the proverbial *glasshouse*. Build the system or process in such a way that it is crystal clear when the system breaks down, who, or what department, is accountable.

Remember how I defined productivity earlier? There is a need to develop a prescription for productivity. Strive to make every function and department within the system as productive as possible. Every activity or task should contribute to achieving the goal of making money. Harness all your resources as efficiently and effectively as possible.

Develop real and lasting operational change. Remember, lead change, don't manage change. Have a passion for what you do and build trust among all team members, both internal and external. Take the principles you will learn in this book and put them to practical use in the everyday life of the organization. Teach the team the benefits of these principles. Reward your team for positive results. Show all your resources, including subcontractors, suppliers, and consultants, how they can increase their revenue by following these steps. Learn their businesses' processes and teach them how to implement these principles. There are many, many things to focus on regarding the organization. Be consistent in the direction you lead your team. Keep the team positive and striving for excellence in everything they do.

4.1 You need a CHAMPION to lead the way.

Achieving operational excellence and continually improving requires a specific focus and leadership. You need an *OPERATIONS CHAMPION* to lead the way. You may be the Champion for a time, but whatever the size of your organization, you need someone to concentrate solely on leading operations. If you are an entrepreneur or business owner, you have numerous things to focus on. Also, operations may not be one of your strengths. The Champion must have a focus and commitment on making the entire organization operationally excellent. They should have a real *PASSION* for creating excellence in every detail of the organization. Like all good leaders, they should possess outstanding character, high integrity, a competitive spirit, an unwavering will to win, and be the best at what the organization produces. The Champion should be an effective leader who excels at systemizing the organization's profitable work and an entrepreneur who has a vision for the organization's future.

I like to say, "Dominate the competition with excellence". The Champion needs to have this kind of mindset. Have each one of your team members read this book. The one who understands and grasps these principles may be your Champion. You may need to hire a consultant who understands how to implement these principles to teach your team, or you may need to hire a new team member Champion from outside the organization. Whichever way you obtain your Champion, you must give them the authority and support to lead and execute change. If the Champion is part of your internal team, provide them with the title of Vice President of Operations or Director of Operations, so the entire team understands the Champion has the proper authority.

The Champion should be responsible for engineering the entire workflow of your system's processes and focus on continuous improvement.

You need a *Champion* to lead the way to Operational Excellence.

4.2 The Right People in the Right Positions.

It is crucial to the success of your organization that you have the right people in the correct positions—hiring and training a new team member, whether internal or external, is incredibly costly. It is even more expensive to *PROPERLY* re-hire and train the right new team member. It is even more costly, yet, and can become disastrous to realize that you have made a bad hire. Your team members are truly the most critical asset the organization has. The time and expense that it takes to learn how to properly recruit, interview, evaluate, hire, train, and place your new team members is undeniably the best money you will ever spend. Look at the total value of an existing team member. For example, the time and expense it will take to recruit, hire, and thoroughly train their replacement. Is that good team member worth a little more compensation to keep them on your team?

Hiring an outstanding consultant who specializes in organizational development is a wise investment. I have worked with Martin Freedland, the President of the Berke Group, throughout my career, achieving excellent results. Martin has been an enormous asset to me in many ways throughout my career. The Berke Group is a leader in the teaching and implementation of organizational development tools and processes. They will help you in hiring great (Bright) and (Allow) nurture them to succeed (Thrive). The Berke Assessment[1] It is a fantastic tool that helps you determine the core competencies and abilities of your current team members and future recruits. Have the entire current internal team take the Berke Assessment so you can identify each team member's strengths and weaknesses. It is a good idea to evaluate and understand the core competencies of your leaders first, and then those of all your team members. The Berke Assessment will provide you with the information you need to determine whether your team members are a proper fit for the positions they hold.

---

[1] The Berke Assessment is a proprietary document administered solely by the Berke Group. All Rights Reserved.

I have found that formal education is not as crucial as *Emotional Intelligence*. Self-control, persistence, and motivation are equally, if not more important than a high I.Q. These attributes create innovative work. Please understand me; having highly educated team members is valuable, but the majority of the extremely successful people that we think of have possessed emotional intelligence, whether they were highly educated or had no formal education at all. Perhaps it explains why 80% of billionaires do not have a college degree.

When you are confident that you have the right people in the correct positions, create and publish an organizational chart so that the entire team can see and understand the organization's reporting structure. A vital issue to keep in mind is that managers should have no more than 3-5 direct reports. This allows for the proper management and growth of every individual. Follow the example of the United States military, which has a transparent chain of command that has been highly successful for over two hundred years. I have been involved with companies that have published organizational charts and those that do not. I believe that you need an understandable organizational chart that clearly outlines the reporting structure and lines of authority to achieve operational excellence within the organization.

Innovative work is always productive and moves the organization closer to generating revenue. Utilize current means, methods, and technology to build a team effectively. Hire and use successful consultants. Put the right people in the correct positions. *IT WILL PAY BENEFITS.*

4.3 Training and Continual Learning.

Be a Lifelong Learner and encourage your team members to do the same. Continue to stretch yourself and your team by attending seminars, lectures, taking new classes, reading articles and books, and so on. You can never get too much knowledge.

We have all heard it said, "Life is like a box of chocolates, you never know what you are going to get."[2] That statement is true; we cannot predict the future. But we also have a lot of experience from the diversity of life and have gained knowledge that needs to be shared and passed along to others. Don't be concerned about how old you are or what your background or past has been. Your successes and failures create knowledge. We all have knowledge that is worthy of sharing. Each one of us has a great deal of experience that can be of benefit to others through training and teaching. Please pay it forward. Help someone else to achieve the knowledge and success that you have gained. Provide opportunities for your team members to continually learn and grow.

---

[2] This quote was made by the character Forrest Gump in the movie titled Forrest Gump. The 1994 film released by Paramount Pictures and directed by Robert Zemeckis and the novel of the same name by Winston Groom.

Offer learning that teaches your team competencies that are related to what you want to accomplish with the organization. Bring in consultants, topical experts, and successful professionals to train your team on the best practices for each function within your organization and its operational processes. Explain to the team that you do not have all the answers, but you do have some of them. Together with a group of experienced advisors and team members, you can obtain a large percentage of the answers. Remember, there is always room for continuous improvement. Exposing your team to the knowledge and successes of others is hugely beneficial.

Create a Learning Organization. A learning organization continually improves and stays profitable and competitive by being *a Lifelong learner.*

Train the team on how to properly and efficiently organize the work of each functional area, ensuring high productivity. The Champion should take responsibility for this training. Eliminate all rework and revamp every step of the current process that is inefficient or unproductive. Each step of the function's process should be based on the Even Flow principles. Document all of the methods of your operation. Begin by creating a high-level process map for each department or functional area, including the workflow of the entire organization and the duration of each function. This will make your *Critical Path* schedule. Then have the members of each function document every specific detail and duration of the tasks needed to complete their operation properly. You may find that these details revise the Critical Path. I will discuss the specific details of how to engineer process maps later in this book. The individuals who perform the work are the best resource for needed changes and improvements in the current process. Once the process improvements have been made, compile the written information on the tasks and steps of the improved process to develop a training manual that serves as a reference guide for the team and a training tool for new team members. Hold each department head responsible for keeping the manual up to date with every process improvement and change.

Keep the entire team informed of your plans, objectives, and past successes. I have found that the more information you can share with your team, the more they are kept engaged and focused on the future goals and objectives. Plus, it keeps them feeling like a team and that they are truly responsible for the organization's results. I have heard from team members many times that not including them in the *State of the Organization* or withholding information on what the organization is planning for the future makes them feel isolated and not part of a true team. I have had great success over the years by holding quarterly team meetings. Hold separate sessions for the internal team and the external team. Please provide them with as much information as necessary, such as initiatives, objectives, process improvements, and achievements.

We gain knowledge from our education and past experiences. Wisdom is taking that knowledge and effectively using it for the future. God tells us to seek wisdom first. It is better than past knowledge. Drawing on the insight that you and others have gained is the best prescription for success in both your personal and professional life.

Chapter 5

Establish Clear, Realistic, and Attainable Goals

To know where you are going, whether in business or life, requires dreams and goals. To get from point A to point B, you need a plan and a map. Not just any plan, but a plan that everyone on the team shares and follows. Everyone needs to be headed in the same direction. Every individual's and department
Goals or objectives must align with the company's overall objectives and the primary goal of generating revenue.

Establish clear, realistic, and *ATTAINABLE* goals. Avoid setting unachievable goals, as this can lead to disillusionment among the team with the plan and your leadership. Set initial goals that are easily achievable, allowing for the establishment and maintenance of proper momentum for success. Early wins keep the team energized and focused on the overall objective. Stay consistent with your goals. Do not be a *flavor-of-the-month manager*. Do not change your direction and long-term goals every month. Set goals that can be achieved within a reasonable timeframe. Six months at a maximum. Some goals may require structured planning for extended periods, but ensure you have specific points in time to track and measure your progress. At Village Homes, we established a three-year improvement plan. The plan outlined detailed, specific improvements we wanted to achieve by the end of year one, year two, and to reach all established improvement goals by the end of year three. We reviewed the status of the goals at the end of each year, and at the end of year three, we established new target goals. We implemented *Quarterly Performance Reviews* specific to each job function, aligning them with both short- and long-term goals. The performance reviews were done by individual job and department, with measurable results specific to each function. Each item on the reviews made it possible to track established milestone results and allowed us to know if we were on track to meet our year-end goals. An essential aspect of performance reviews is posting and reporting the results. We also ranked individuals by their results. It has been proven that when you measure results, they improve. When results are reported and posted, they continue to improve. We also established a *Bonus Program* that was directly tied to the Performance Review results. An example of a specific Performance Review is for the function of a Construction Superintendent. This function was responsible for the overall management of the construction of new homes. We focused on five main areas of responsibility for the Construction Superintendent. I called them the *Critical Few* activities of the job function. They are:

ON TIME – (Production Schedule). Measures the variance in days from the original (baseline) production schedule, both positive days and negative days.

ON BUDGET – (Construction Budget). Measure the variance in dollars from the original at-start construction budget.

WITH QUALITY – (Pre-Closing Management Quality Walk). Measure the quality scores from the Pre-closure Management Quality Walk inspection checklist.

CUSTOMER SATISFACTION – (Customer Satisfaction Survey Scores). Measure the customer satisfaction scores of the customer survey taken at closing.

SAFETY – (Safety Scores). Measure the safety scores (at least two random safety inspections per home) of each safety inspection checklist.

Identify the critical few for each job function, then create the Quarterly Performance Review. Implement performance reviews for each individual within the organization. Also, consider implementing an annual profit-sharing plan. This is another way to keep the team focused on the goal of increasing profitability.

How do you establish your goals so that they have the most significant impact on Making Money? A good place to start is to inspect variances. Variances are deviations from the original expectation. Identify your primary variances and establish processes to improve or eliminate them. Elimination of costly variances can have a drastic impact on increasing profitability. Variances can be either positive or negative. A production schedule variance in homebuilding can be either ahead of schedule (positive variance) or behind schedule (unfavorable variance). In this example, both positive and negative variances ***always incur costs*** and negatively impact profitability. I will explain this in more detail later in a future chapter.

Chapter 6

The Theory of Constraints [Goldratt]

The Theory of Constraints (T.O.C.), which Dr. Goldratt introduced, is the "ultimate science of business and organizations"[Goldratt 2004]. T.O.C. includes proven principles and methodologies that optimize production and process techniques that maximize workflow and profitability. I will share real-life examples of how T.O.C. principles were used to streamline and create processes that dramatically increased profitability. "There are only two ways these principles *will not work*: 1. There is no demand for your products and/or services. 2. You are determined not to change". [Goldratt 2004]

6.1 THROUGHPUT, INVENTORY, and OPERATIONAL EXPENSE

There are three key measurements that you must continually keep at the forefront of the operations improvement journey. These terms are fundamental in the way they are worded, and everything in the organization is covered by one of these three measurements. *IT IS THAT SIMPLE.* The terms and their definitions are stated below.

THROUGHPUT: Is the rate at which the system generates money through SALES, not production. If you produce something but do not sell it, it is not Throughput.

Throughput = Sales. Not just a contract, order, or a deposit, but a product and/or service completed by the system and the total revenue (money) received.

INVENTORY: Is all the money the system has invested in purchasing things that it intends to sell. Inventory is not just unsold finished goods, but it includes everything your business owns, including depreciation and the potential sale price.

OPERATIONAL EXPENSE: Is all the money the system spends to turn Inventory into Throughput. Money is spent to produce output. The carrying cost of Inventory is Operational Expense. Example: Warranty Service labor after Throughput is Operational Expense. (Customer Service Dept.)

Another way to define these measurements is to say that they represent money coming in (Throughput), money stuck within the system (Inventory), and money going out (Operational Expense). You will notice that each definition contains the word *Money*. To maximize profitability, you must improve the entire system. Remember, a chain is only as strong as its weakest link. One area of improvement in your business is not enough. One improved measurement alone is not enough. You must positively change at least one of the other measurements as well. Many processes or areas can be enhanced to increase profitability and throughput, while decreasing inventory and/or expenses, ultimately leading to increased sales. ***The focus should be on increasing throughput while simultaneously reducing both Inventory and Operational Expenses.*** The objective is not to improve one measurement in isolation. I am talking about improving the entire workflow system or organization. Not just one area or one department.

Please give it some thought. See if you can place any function of your organization under one of these three measurements. You need to focus on this methodology as the foundation of your thought process as you embark on the journey of achieving operational excellence and increased profitability.

The information contained in this chapter is essential to achieving operational excellence. This is a brief chapter, but it is imperative.

---

[3] Most of the information and text contained in this chapter is from Dr. Eliyahu M. Goldratt presented in the book *The Goal a Process of Ongoing Improvement.*

Chapter 7

Financial Measurements

You need simplistic, and *REAL* financial measurements. Your current measurements may be misleading you. What I mean is having the old mentality that causes us to save pennies while sacrificing dollars.

Net Profit, Return on Investment, and Cash Flow are simple but needed financial measurements. Continued positive results in these three measurements are crucial for knowing that your organization is generating a profit. You want to see all three of these measurements increase all the time. One measurement, such as Net Profit, is not enough to accurately measure. You need another measurement, too. Like, how much money did you contribute to make money in Net Profit? You also need R.O.I. (Return on Investment). You also need a Cash Flow measurement. The Cash Flow measurement is a financial measurement that can determine the organization's survival.

We need to forget the outdated "standard cost accounting" rules, such as:
- "Production Efficiencies."
- "Economies of Scale."
- "Costs," etc.

Your financial numbers are likely accurate, but your thought process may be flawed. Again, thinking that we are saving pennies, but in reality, we are sacrificing additional dollars of profitability. Increasing throughput should always be fully considered when making decisions about financial measurements. Always consider your system's constraints when determining your throughput. Picture an Hourglass in your mind. Your ultimate throughput is determined by the function or task that has the least capacity. You need to shift your thinking away from obsolete Cost Accounting and toward Throughput Accounting. Focus on constraints, not costs. I will discuss these principles in more detail later.

As I stated earlier, having baselines (Such as Maps, Budgets, and schedules) to start your measurements is very important. If you do not have a starting point, you cannot track the improvements. Whatever financial measurements you use, remember to keep them simple and ensure they track the results you truly need. Another area of focus to ensure the gross profitability continually increases is to check the *Gross Margin* at several points during the workflow process. In the homebuilding business, you need at least three key points to check the Gross Margin.
1. *At the point of writing the contract or sales agreement.* The buyer may choose to include standard options or special requests in the product, which can impact the gross margin.

2. *At the point of starting production.* The buyer may have purchased upgrades or additional options to the product after initiating the contract or sales agreement (Design Center). Also, there may have been site-specific costs, etc.
3. *At the point of production completion.* The buyer may have made additional changes after the start. Additionally, there may have been variances that affect the gross margin.

Again, any variance that hurts the gross margin needs to be improved or eliminated. Gross Margin is a key financial measurement.

Another key financial measurement to focus on is the *Breakeven Point.* The breakeven point of your organization is defined in simple terms as the point within your fiscal year at which all the yearly indirect costs have been met, such as salaries, utility bills, mortgages or rent, equipment costs, insurance, and other similar expenses. If you can increase productivity so you can reach the breakeven point earlier in the fiscal year, all of your revenue, except for the direct material costs to produce the product, drops *RIGHT TO THE BOTTOM LINE*. One example of this, and there are many, many more, is the construction superintendent. Let us start by saying that an experienced superintendent can PROFESSIONALLY manage fifteen homes under construction at one time. The current production schedule has a duration of six months. That provides two inventory turns per year. 2 inventory turns x 15 homes under construction = 30 new homes a superintendent manages and produces in a year. Now, let's say through process improvement and operational excellence, we were able to decrease the production schedule to a four-month duration. This would provide three inventory turns per year, without increasing the superintendent's salary or workload. It now looks like this. 3 inventory turns x 15 homes under construction = 45 new homes a superintendent manages and produces in a year. It is like a car shifting gears. With each gear shift (process improvement), the car increases speed, but the engine can still turn at the same RPMs. The Construction Superintendent example helps move up the breakeven point, and the *ADDITIONAL GROSS PROFIT* drops right to the bottom line. The net profitability increases exponentially with each completed sale beyond the breakeven point. You can imagine the positive financial impact it would have throughout the entire organization by increasing the annual inventory turns. Reducing the duration that it takes to produce a product is a *HUGE BENEFIT* to obtaining operational excellence. This is a real-life example of what was and can be achieved.

There are many more financial measurements you can use. However, remember to consider the measurements you are using and how they are being applied. You want to show improvement in the entire system, not just in one or two isolated areas.

I have covered several important topics, but there are many specific components still to be discussed on our journey to achieve Operational Excellence.

Chapter 8

Organizational Balance Using Even Flow Principles

WE spoke about personal balance, now I want to address organizational balance. I will discuss a few topics that may challenge your current beliefs and what you have been taught in the past. Please read the entire chapter and give the information some thought before you make hasty judgments. I need to discuss a balanced system or workflow at this point so that the remaining chapters will be more transparent and more cohesive.

"Most of what we have been taught about business causes us to make decisions about our businesses that cause the organization to be inefficient." [Goldratt 2004] We have been taught that a balanced workflow is when the capacity of each resource is balanced with the market demand. This is not true, and in fact, this type of organization is very inefficient. Think about what I just said for a moment.

"We MUST balance the overall output and flow of product so that it will be just less than the market demand." [Goldratt 2004] An example in the homebuilding business would be to set your system to produce homes

just below your monthly or annual home closing rate. Not written contracts, sales agreements, or deposits.

Remember, Throughput is a produced sale. *"DO NOT HAVE A BALANCED SYSTEM BUT, RATHER HAVE A SYSTEM THAT BALANCES THE FLOW OF PRODUCT THROUGH THE SYSTEM WITH DEMAND FROM THE MARKET."* [Goldratt 2004] Balance flow, not capacity.

A process or workflow is inefficient if all resources are working at 100% capacity all the time. As American managers, this is a complex concept to comprehend and accept. We have been taught that every resource should be available and functioning at all times. This is incorrect thinking and is highly inefficient. This type of thinking produces increased inventory and expenses. Let me give you an example. Imagine that you are the manager of several teams at various work centers. Standard work hours are 8:00 a.m. to 5:00 p.m., with a one-hour lunch break from 12:00 p.m. to 1:00 p.m. It is 11:20 a.m., and you stop by one of the work centers to find all of the workers reading the newspaper, playing cards, etc., but none of them are working. What is your first thought? EVERYONE GET TO WORK!

This may be wrong thinking. Suppose the work center has more capacity than another work center downstream in the workflow system. In that case, having all those workers produce all the time creates inventory and operational expenses, which we have already learned is not an efficient use of resources. ***"Can*** *we assume that making people work and making money are the same thing"*? [Goldratt 2004] You may need to shift some of the idle workers to another CONSTRAINED area to increase capacity and thus increase throughput. *Idle Time* on a non-constrained task or function is a *GOOD THING*. Idle time is a cost to increase throughput. Some percentage of time on a non-constrained resource should be idle time. You cannot measure the capacity of a resource in isolation. The resource's actual production capacity depends on its location within the system. Remember to balance the FLOW, not capacity. Let me give you another simplistic example. The numbers listed below represent the number of units in capacity that each work center can produce within the system's workflow cycle. Assume the work centers must be placed in this dependent order to produce throughput properly.

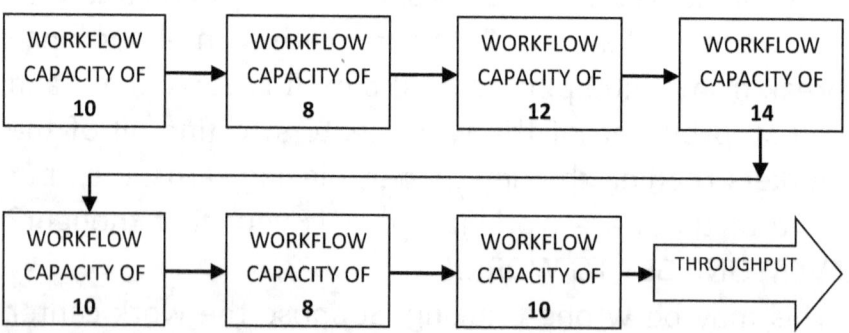

In this example, what is the maximum throughput this system can achieve?

The answer is eight units. Although the largest unit capacity of a work center within the system is 14, the maximum throughput capacity of the system is determined by the constrained work center, which has an eight-unit capacity. To increase the throughput of the system, you will need to either reduce the workload or add more resources to the constrained work center, thereby increasing its capacity. If the throughput of the system is eight units, every other work center that has a capacity exceeding eight units should have *Idle Time*. If they don't, the system is inefficient, resulting in unnecessary inventory and operational expenses. Let's use the same example I used above, but let's add the inventory that this system will produce if all work centers operate at full capacity continuously.

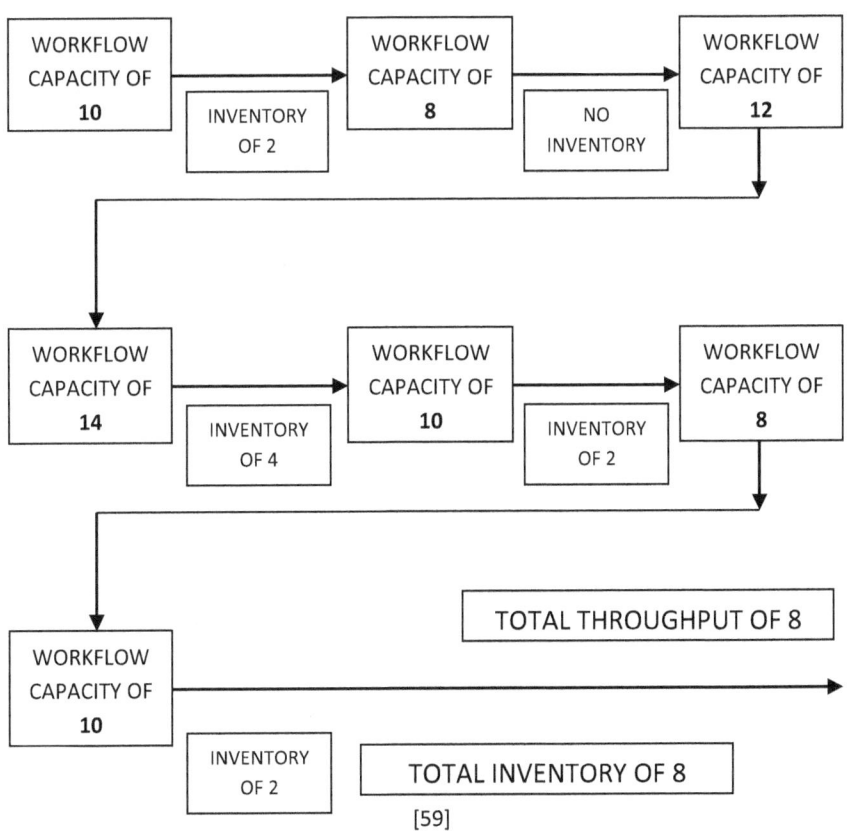

This system will only produce a throughput of 8 units. Still, if all work centers operate at maximum capacity all the time, the system will accumulate a total of 8 additional units of costly inventory that will not become throughput.
This is not Operational Excellence.

These principles should be applied throughout the entire system workflow and also drill down to the detailed workflow of each function or step within every individual process.

8.1 Even Flow

Each task within a process, which makes up the overall workflow, should follow *EVEN FLOW* principles. Every task is completed at a pace determined by the constrained activity, regardless of its location within the process. Like the *Beat of a Drum,* it should be a consistent pace. If market demand increases, the pace or drumbeat should be increased at an incremental and systematic rate. Not at large jumps in the release of work (Inventory) into the system. If homebuilders had based their estimated growth or system needs on the number of homes closed, rather than the number of contracts written or deposits taken, many homebuilding organizations would not have filed for bankruptcy during the 2008 economic downturn. Even Flow principles should also be applied when developing new land or purchasing completed, buildable lots. Everything that the organization does should be done with even flow methodology. Do not overstretch or spread yourself too thin. Have balance throughout the entire organization.

Create an assembly line-type system that encompasses every department, function, or task within the entire organization. If the constrained activity's capacity to produce is less than (just under) the market demands, the system will not make the desired maximum throughput. Have (something like) physical links between functions. Create a *Chain* in the assembly line. Picture in your mind an automobile assembly line. Every activity in the assembly line depends on the preceding activity being 100% complete with the required quality before it is allowed to proceed to the next work center. If a defect is discovered, the hypothetical Chord is pulled, stopping the entire assembly line until the defect is corrected, allowing the assembly line to be started again. Correcting a defect should always be the top priority. A delay in the assembly line is extraordinarily costly and will **always** negatively affect the throughput. Resources down the line will have to add extra capacity to make up for lost time and deal with the delay. Let me give you an example of the potential cost to your organization for one day of delayed throughput. The homebuilder I was working with at the time was closing approximately 500 new homes a year. They had several assembly lines producing products simultaneously. At an average of $350,000.00 in revenue per closing, which produced 175 million dollars in annual revenue. Divide the total annual revenue by 365 days, and in this case, the cost of one day lost in throughput is *$479,452.05. That is a per-day potential loss*. Your team will have to work much longer and/or on more complex tasks to make up for the lost time and offset the delay. Plug in your numbers. Annual throughput in revenue, divided by 365 days a year, equals the potential loss of revenue per day due to delayed throughput. That is **HUGE DOLLARS**, no matter what size the organization. The math never lies. 2+2 always equals 4. Show this simple example to everyone associated with the organization, especially your external team members. Show them their annual number of delay days and the cost impact of those delays when they come looking for a price increase. The numbers will likely indicate that they owe you money and that they are fortunate to be still utilizing your services.

The non-float tasks of the workflow process schedule are equal to the *Critical Path* of the system. Similarly, the constrained activity always sets the start pace or release of new work into the system. In homebuilding, the start pace would be starting construction on a new home (Inventory released into the system). Release new starts based on the optimal pace or capacity of the constraint. Remember, to increase the start pace, you must increase the capacity of the constrained activity, which will ultimately improve throughput. It is pretty simple.

8.2 Process Control Manager

The Process Control Manager (PCM) collaborates with the Champion to ensure that each work process flow continues to run smoothly and efficiently. The PCM should thoroughly understand and be familiar with the implementation of the information contained in this book. Traditionally, in the homebuilding business, the Process Control Manager has focused on the portion of the system responsible for constructing new homes and all activities related to that function. However, *EVERY* critical path activity within the system's workflow should be monitored daily. If you are genuinely applying Even Flow principles, critical activities are occurring daily throughout the organization. In homebuilding, for example, this includes the vital activities of the entire system, from property acquisition to warranty service, and every activity in between. Depending on the size of your organization, you may need several Process Control Managers, including those for pre-product start, product production, and post-product completion, among others. Perhaps one Process Control Manager can oversee your entire system. Still, they must manage the schedule to ensure the proper completion of every critical path activity every day, throughout the whole workflow.

The primary function of the Process Control Manager is to make sure that even flow is maintained throughout the entire system. If the system's throughput needs to be increased or decreased due to market changes, it must be done incrementally, and both the Process Control Manager(s) and the Champion must be involved.

For example, let's suppose a homebuilding organization plans to open a new community of newly designed homes. The company will have to go through the land acquisition, entitlement, and land development stages. Also, new architectural designs, engineering, and the cost of the latest products will have to be determined and approved. New Sales and Marketing materials will need to be created and implemented. Once the process has been started, the Grand Opening date for the community and the latest product offering is set based on the master schedule of the entire workflow process.

Like all entrepreneurs, I am a firm believer in the benefits of *Speed to Market with a* product offering. But, unlike most entrepreneurs' thought process, the Product Offering Date MUST be moved back if particular milestone (critical path) dates are not achieved as originally scheduled and planned in the workflow schedule. Suppose delays have accumulated during the workflow process, and the product offering date remains unchanged. In that case, the VISE EFFECT will occur, and your team will suffer, as will the quality of both your product and your process. I will explain what I mean by the Vise Effect. Let's assume in the homebuilding business that some scheduled critical path milestone dates have not been achieved along the assembly line as initially planned for the Grand Opening of a new community, and the executive management of the organization is not willing to push back the opening date (which is generally the case). Several functions, such as purchasing (trade bid and contracting) and the actual production of new products, are not given the proper time to follow the prescribed process, schedule, or produce the product with the required quality. Thus, the vice effect and the latter activities in the assembly line get squeezed.

The Process Control Manager (PCM) is also responsible for releasing new product onto the assembly line based on even flow at the system's current optimal pace. The PCM may need to monitor multiple workflow processes simultaneously. When starting new homes on the assembly line for construction, the PCM controls the start pace based on an even flow and the capacity of the constrained activity. The term *'Start Slot' is used to ensure that even flow slots are maintained on a daily or weekly basis and starts are not missed, thereby preventing* uneven production by the system. The throughput requirement determines the start slots. For example, if the throughput requirement is 156 new homes closed annually, the even flow start slots of a six-day work week would look like this. One hundred fifty-six closings divided by 52 weeks in one year equals three starts per week. The start slots would be one start on

Monday, one starts on Wednesday, and one starts on Friday, to achieve even flow start results.

The start of a new home requires that specific necessary and needed information is complete, such as building plans, building permit, foundation type, selections, purchase orders, etc. The term *Start Pack* is used to encompass all the required information and documentation. Once the Start Pack is complete, the home can be assigned a start date and scheduled to go on the assembly line. Ensure all Start Packs are fully complete and released (including all customer selections) before the assigned start date. The process allows for changes to be made post-start, provided they are made according to specific cut-off dates. If a home is allowed to start without the required information, you can expect delays in the process while waiting for the needed information. **Remember, the financial impact of just one day's delay can have.** Create *Queue Start Packs*, which will become Speculation (Spec) Homes or Move-in Ready Homes, in case one of the pre-slotted start packs is not entirely ready to be started on time. Alternatively, consider moving a future pre-contracted Start Slot forward if the fully completed Start Pack is available. The PCM should constantly monitor the pre-start process to ensure that there are adequate completed Start Packs that can be slotted for even flow starts. I have found that having a *Weekly Starts Meeting* is highly effective. All key personnel involved in the pre-start process should be required to attend the start meeting. The PCM should run the Weekly Starts Meeting. Be disciplined. Hold everyone accountable. Always adhere to the rules of the process. Anything less is not operational excellence.

The PCM is also responsible for keeping the assembly line on schedule. If delays occur in the workflow, the PCM is responsible for effectively managing capacity to minimize the impact on throughput. All delays must be handled daily. *NEVER* rely on your resources to manage their capacity when it comes to your processes. If a resource offers excess capacity, it *MUST* be managed and directed only by the PCM. The PCM can view all the assembly lines and determine where additional resource capacity is needed most. I will discuss the handling of schedules and resources in more detail in the Schedules chapter. The PCM must have total authority to manage each assembly line schedule.

The PCM should also assist in *Supply Chain Management, along with other managers, such as the Purchasing Team*. The PCM needs to monitor the production schedule to ensure that necessary materials are properly distributed at the correct time. Excess material deliveries result in increased inventory and operational expenses. *Just-in-time delivery* principles must be established and maintained. Create just-in-time material delivery, just when it is needed. This is another aspect of creating efficient operations in multiple areas of the system.

An essential aspect of the PCM's function is the ability to accurately monitor the system's schedule on at least a daily basis. Depending on the type of organization, the PCM may need the information even more frequently than daily. Utilize the latest technology to deliver the necessary information. Implement a computerized process that enables authorized personnel to accurately update the schedule at the designated time(s). An automated information system allows access to current data at any time. Absolute, accurate, and timely schedule updates are crucial for the PCM to complete its function efficiently. I will discuss the PCM further in the chapter that deals specifically with the work schedule.

Chapter 9

The Business Plan: "Plan the Attack Then Attack the Plan"

I stated earlier that without a plan and a map, it is virtually impossible to get to where you want to go efficiently and with productivity. However, the plan must be clear, realistic, and achievable. The plan can have objectives that stretch the system's resources, but it must not be over-stretched, and it must adhere to even flow principles as discussed earlier. The system must always focus on achieving productive and efficient operations. Remember, efficient equals excellent.

Let me explain what I mean by *"Plan the Attack and Attack the Plan."*[4]. The business plan needs a realistic current baseline(s) to be able to track results and any variances from the original target(s). A good place to start creating the business plan is by reviewing the total closed sales from the previous fiscal year. Remember, a *sale* is not truly complete until the product is delivered and the revenue is received. Also, the business plan should reflect current market conditions. The market may be drastically different from the previous year. The business plan should include projected *Sales, Starts (production), and Closings* on a weekly and monthly

---
[4] Quotation from Scott Chaikin circa 2001

basis. The results should be tracked and matched to the business plan on a daily, weekly, and monthly basis to ensure the plan is being achieved. Please do not wait to track the actual outcome at the end of the month; instead, track it regularly throughout the month. If you are behind on projections, it will be too late to achieve the planned results. Every function throughout the system should be performed with the mindset of maintaining even flow. Hold *Business Plan Meetings,* which provide plan updates at least once a month. However, I prefer weekly meetings so that appropriate management can be addressed promptly. Have the department heads of each functional area report, take responsibility, and accept accountability for the actual results of the business plan. Like each meeting the organization holds, the meeting should always be productive, have a timed, detailed, and specific agenda, and hold the appropriate people accountable. This methodology can also be implemented on a workflow process-by-process or project-by-project basis. You need a realistic business plan, schedule, and budget that can be tracked with actual results, at a minimum, on a monthly basis.

The greatest enemy of a good plan is the dream of a perfect one. Strategic business planning should be ongoing and continually evolving. Do not get bogged down with trying to create the ideal plan. Select a few strategic goals, such as sales, starts, and closings, for example, or, if the plan is project-based, focus on being on time, on budget, and with quality. Please keep it simple. You do not need to overanalyze where you are going with your business or project. Select a few key metrics to track your progress and move forward with the plan. Establish short-term and longer-term objectives. Get the momentum started by having some early wins and increasing the longer-term objectives as the organization improves. Remember, create consistent long-term goals. Consider targeting positive one-year, two-year, and three-year objective results. As strategic planning improves, incorporate the enhancements into the longer-term objectives. Try to maintain the direction that the organization is going. Frequent changes in direction can confuse the team. At the end of each year, evaluate how the organization has performed against its objectives and establish revised targets as necessary.

Listed below are a few simple examples of homebuilding business plan tools. Choose the tools and reports that help you to monitor key results best, but keep it simple.
- Quick Pro Forma Tool (Land & Build).
- Backlog Predicted Margin Analysis.
- Proposed Budget. (Track Variances).
- Direct Overhead Projections (Site).
- Product Cost Analysis.
- Projected Sales Contracts/Starts/Closings Calendar Forecast.

Having a detailed budget of your finances is also an integral part of your planning. Create a budget for both your business and personal life. Create a realistic budget by using the most accurate data available. Break the budget into specific details by department and by function. The objective is to spend as little money as possible without hindering the ability for ongoing process improvement. Be smart with the money and spend where the costs will improve productivity. Have a tight budget and track your variances closely, both positive and negative. Including too much cushion or too many contingencies in the budget leaves room for unnecessary expenses and hinders the achievement of operational excellence. Have one line item per major category of contingency expense to cover the potential overruns, but track all unaccounted-for expenditures. Do not add contingencies to every line item, as that will hinder the accurate representation of the budget. You want to have the mindset of doing more with less. *Bootstrapping* is never a bad thing. Again, if there are variances from the original plan, that is where you should focus your process improvement initiatives. The growth will be more systematic and much easier to adjust to changes in the market.

Another essential part of the plan should be the projected monthly Profit and Loss portion. This report identifies areas for necessary improvement. If the projected profit is not being met, determine the cause and rectify the issue. The primary goal is always to generate revenue.

Include as many team members in the business and budget planning as you deem appropriate. I would highly recommend including key leadership and holding them responsible for *Plan compliance*. I have witnessed, time and again, the achievement of the original business plan when the entire management team is included and held accountable.

You can never plan your future based on your past. Things are constantly changing. Plan where you want to go, but be prepared to make changes. Be flexible. Learn and improve every day. Always ask God to direct your steps and give you wisdom. He is waiting for you to ask.

Chapter 10

Process Engineering and Mapping

Having an accurate, detailed, and readable map is necessary if you hope to get from point A to point Z most efficiently and productively. ***The definition of Process Mapping is a workflow diagram (map) to bring forth a clearer understanding of a process or a series of parallel processes***. If your organization already has a highly detailed workflow map with an identified critical path, where each process is fully documented, that's fantastic! However, if you don't (which most organizations don't), you need this tool to determine your baseline workflow and identify areas for improvement.

I have worked with some large companies that produce hundreds of millions in annual revenue. Some companies have had excellent maps and process documentation, and some have had very little, if any. But every company I have been associated with has had much-needed room for improvement and could be much more profitable. There is **NO WAY** that operational excellence can be obtained without having a highly efficient, productive, and detailed workflow map that contains every step that takes place from beginning to end.

Process Mapping refers to activities involved in defining what a business entity does, who is responsible, for what duration an activity or process should be completed, and how the success of a process can be determined.

I would strongly recommend that the management team of the organization set aside time to come together and review the existing map (if one exists) or to initiate the process of engineering and mapping the organization's entire workflow, step by step, from start to finish. Include someone from each functional area who is familiar with every step of their process. Also, include a few of your key trade partners in engineering the workflow map. They will provide valuable insights from their perspective on areas of the workflow that can be improved to increase efficiency and productivity. Depending on the magnitude of the workflow processes, there may be a need for several meetings to complete the workflow mapping. If you do not have the necessary people at each meeting, you are wasting time; therefore, the team must realize the importance of these mapping meetings. Complete the map engineering as quickly as possible. Once you have established the meeting(s) with the correct people needed for workflow engineering and mapping, you can begin.

I have provided a simple example of a cross-functional process map to illustrate its structure. There are many

Proven Principles and Methodologies to Achieve Increased Profitability

types of process maps, but I have found that when dealing with multiple departments or functional areas and multiple assembly lines operating simultaneously, this example is particularly effective. The actual completed process map will be significantly larger, encompassing many more individual processes.

10.1 EXAMPLE OF A CROSS-FUNCTIONAL PROCESS MAP

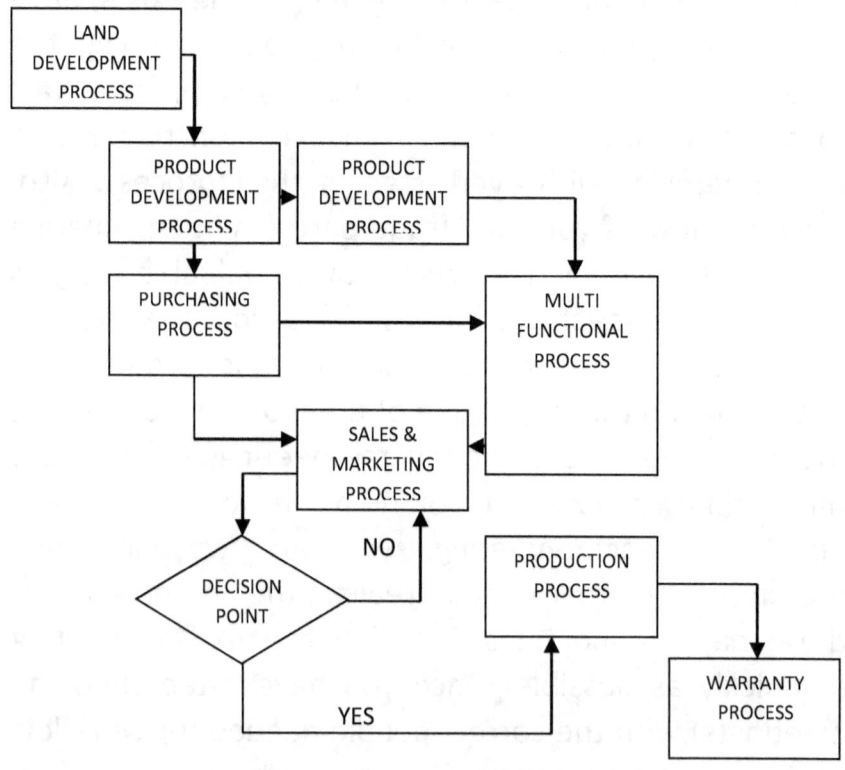

Here are some ideas that can be utilized in engineering the workflow (system) process map. I suggest using large Post-it notes for engineering the workflow map. They can be easily relocated to another location if changes are made to the workflow. Use different color Post-its for each department or functional area's processes. Use white Post-its to mark each milestone activity and turn them on their side to create a diamond shape when decision points occur. Find a large whiteboard or select a clean wall to create the workflow map. Use a sheet of butcher paper that is long and wide enough to provide ample room to place the processes and the connection lines necessary for the map. Assign one member of the workflow mapping team to be responsible for documenting and maintaining the map.

Create a process map for **every** area of the organization. Department by Department, Area by Area, Process by Process. Map the entire workflow from start to finish. Arrange the processes in a dependent order, utilizing their full capacity and considering the current maximum (longest, not average) duration. Organizing the process in sequence, from start to finish, and so on. There may be several lines (branches) where processes coincide. Determine the milestone processes that must be completed before initiating any subsequent activities. Create a *high-level* workflow map to begin with. Do not get bogged down with every detail of specific activities or tasks at first. Be sure to eliminate rework loops if possible. Move the rework activity to the proper location in the workflow so the workflow is not going backwards. Another department or functional area may have already completed the activity, preventing it from having to be revisited in a previous functional area. Remember, try to structure the system using a model of

an assembly line, where every step is completed in a dependent order. Have the Department Managers understand the process of their upline and downline work centers (departments). Avoid including unnecessary quality control inspection points. As I discussed earlier, create a culture where everyone associated with the organization is involved in quality control and everyone is held accountable for ensuring that no work moves down the line with a known defect. Create a culture where it is safe and necessary to *pull the Cord* to stop the assembly line until the defect is appropriately addressed and corrected.

Next, determine the systems' (workflows') *Critical Path*. This part of mapping the workflow is essential. You *MUST* identify each process that *CANNOT* experience a delay. If a delay occurs in a critical path process or activity, it will negatively affect the projected completed throughput rate. Again, if critical path process dates are not met and the original completion date is not extended due to the delay, the Vise Effect will occur.

Once the high-level workflow map has been accurately completed, with each process identified by its proper duration and the critical path of the system established, the details of every task can be documented. Have the department heads of each functional area take responsibility for ensuring their teams document every detailed step involved in completing their processes. Once the **detailed** workflow map is complete, hold each functional area's team accountable to keep the map accurate and up to date. If future changes and improvements are made to the workflow map, a Map Change Process must be established to ensure that changes are not made in isolation and that the entire organization is informed of the change.

You will now have a current, clear, and orderly workflow map that can serve as a baseline to track any deviations from the anticipated workflow schedule. Variances are always areas that require attention and are typically areas in need of improvement. The workflow map can serve as a valuable training tool, enabling all team members to understand the entire organization's workflow system.

Chapter 11

Constraints

Properly dealing with constrained activities is crucial to the system's ability to increase throughput and, consequently, sales and profitability. **A constraint in this case is described as the current slowest activity or task in the workflow process or system.** Any process can only move as fast as its slowest function or task. The first thing to do is to locate the worst constraint, eliminate that constraint, then locate the following most significant constraint, eliminate that constraint, move on to the third, and so on. Identify the activity with the most extensive backlog (work in process) waiting ahead of the following resource. You may have a hunch where to start looking for the constraints. Where in the system have you experienced delays (variances) due to insufficient capacity? Additionally, solicit input and experiences from the individuals who work in the constrained areas. The team will be quick to voice where they are *feeling pain* in the process. Look at both internal resources and external resources that provide work in process (capacity to the system). Also, use accurate computer data to help determine and identify the constraints.

In the construction of production homes, the activity that always seems to be one of the most constrained is framing. I believe there are two main reasons why this occurs. There are not enough framers to meet the needed capacity, and the framing activity typically has one of the longest durations. This may sound intuitive to most home builders, but many organizations are resistant to common sense.

There should be at least one constrained activity in every process within the workflow system. The constrained activity dictates both inventory and throughput. To increase the capacity of the workflow system is to increase the capacity **OF ONLY** the constrained activities. The constrained activity is not necessarily a bad thing. However, its capacity must equal market demand. If the market demand increases, the capacity of the constraint **MUST** increase. Please ensure that the constraints are not violated; their capacity should be greater than or equal to the demand. If there are delays (variances) in a current process, determine the cause.

The constrained activity (or resource) should always be at full capacity. You cannot recover lost production time elsewhere in the workflow system. The lost time on a constrained activity is lost time **FOREVER**.

"There is hidden capacity within the system because some of your thinking is incorrect". [Goldratt 2004] Remember, I discussed that a non-constrained activity will have excess capacity. Again, the definitions of a constrained and a non-constrained activity are:

A constraint is any activity or resource whose capacity is equal to or less than the demand placed upon it.

Non-Constraint - is any activity or resource whose capacity is greater than the demand placed upon it.

Let me discuss a few ways we can increase the throughput of a constrained activity.
- Move the extra resource (capacity) from a non-constrained activity to a constrained activity to make it faster.
- Distribute the workload of a constrained activity to increase its speed.
- Modify the organization's workflow process to facilitate the movement or distribution of the constraint.
- By cutting the non-constrained activities workload in half, it reduces overall cycle times, which increases inventory turns.

Check the throughput on the constrained activities once the capacity improvements have been implemented. Once the upgrades are satisfactory, you can begin to address the following most significant constraint. The objective is to have a workflow system that is structured to produce fast, efficient, and high-quality results, thereby increasing profitability.

If you are the organization's owner, do not let yourself become a constraint in the system. Run your organization; do not let it run you. Do not be a part of the process; lead it.

11.1 Establish a Work Routine

Continue to develop the even flow mindset. **Every activity** must be conducted at the system's optimal pace. Identify the critical few activities within each functional area that must occur on a daily, weekly, or monthly basis to maintain the desired throughput. Develop work routines or habits. For example, after building custom homes for fifteen years, I transitioned into the production home building arena. I started as a builder or superintendent at one production home builder, where I effectively learned the fundamentals of production homebuilding. I had already mastered the technical aspects of building a house. Still, in that position, I learned very quickly that there was a need to establish a work routine that would allow me to accomplish what activities I then named the Critical Few, which I needed to complete each day. My critical few activities included managing the production schedules, inspecting each house's activities for completion and quality, dealing with all variances, both budget and schedule, answering and managing all questions the resources might have, Home Owner Orientation Walks, and making sure that the construction area complied with all applicable rules and regulations, including job site safety. This is why I mentioned earlier that an experienced superintendent can effectively manage only about fifteen houses under construction at a time.

As a production home superintendent, I would start my workday by conducting a quick drive-by of each house under construction to ensure that the proper resources scheduled to work that day had arrived. If the appropriate resource(s) were not available, I would make a note of it and proceed to the next house. Once that was completed, I would go to my field office to contact any no-shows to verify if they were going to meet the schedule. After that, I would start walking through each house in detail. I termed this management walk *Every Room, Every House, Every Day*. This is when I inspected the previous day's activities for total completion and quality, and also spoke with the ongoing resources about the project and schedule. If there were variances from the desired outcome of my inspection, I would contact the affected resource immediately by phone or radio to address the situation. I would take notes of the information obtained during each house's inspection. Each resource quickly became a quality and completion inspector themselves because they all knew that I would inspect their work and hold them accountable for any defect immediately. This is one of the reasons why, if done correctly, speed **DOES NOT** produce poor quality. If proper Inspections and accountability are made every day, the resources will learn that their work is more profitable if done correctly the first time. If other resources contacted me by radio during the walk, needing me to come by the house they were working on, I would ask them if it was urgent. If it were urgent, I would stop in the middle of my inspection and address their issue. If it were not urgent, I would tell them I was on my daily management walk and that I would address the issue when I arrived at the house they were working on. In a short period, they learned that if their problem were not urgent, they would not call and wait for me to come by. This eliminated unnecessary interruptions. Once I had completed walking and managing every house in detail, I would return to the field office to update the production schedule with accurate and current information from the notes I had taken. We were using centralized computer production scheduling, which was sent to the PCM and each resource daily, containing updated and current schedule information. No matter what the interruption, I knew that I had time to pick up where I left off and complete my daily critical few. The routine I established allowed me to complete my critical few without stress in four to five hours each day, which gave me time to attend weekly construction meetings, senior management community inspections, and random management safety inspections. These weekly meetings and inspections allowed me to identify areas where improvements were needed. One special benefit of having a work routine was that I had extra time throughout the week to schedule unanticipated appointments with buyers to meet with them at their new homes. They loved those opportunities, and it helped make my customer satisfaction scores outstanding. Within a very short time, I had established a workable routine that was accepted by everyone involved.

Again, I give all the credit and glory to Christ. Because of His favor and the wisdom He gave me to establish a daily work routine, I was able to achieve my daily critical few and consistently produce outstanding results.

Chapter 12

Schedule(s)

Once you have completed the process engineering and mapping of the entire workflow, including dependent events, durations, and the critical path, establish the overall detailed Master Schedule of the whole system and all necessary sub-schedules for each work center or process. Have each functional area create its schedule, keeping the overall Master Schedule in mind. Hopefully, you have identified some of the worst-constrained tasks, which will help you determine the required capacity of each work center and the entire system. Remember, do not consider the cost of one work center in isolation. You want to increase throughput while decreasing both inventory and operational expense. The entire organization's or project's overall workflow schedule must have a clearly defined total duration from start to finish. Every schedule within the organization should be established using the *Critical Path Method* (CPM).

It is vitally essential that processes are established to allow every schedule within the entire system to be updated daily with completely accurate and current information. The designated team member of each functional area should be responsible for accurate updates of their individual schedule information and then transmitting it to the PCM each day. The easiest way to accomplish this is to create each schedule using a computer system and scheduling software. There are many scheduling software programs on the market today to choose from, but I have found that *Primavera*.[5] The product offers everything needed to create an accurate, automated schedule that can be easily updated and transmitted daily. Additionally, the computer system must be designed to track all schedule delays and variance data. All updated schedule data should be transmitted to and received by the Process Control Manager (PCM) daily for analysis and management, thereby minimizing delays and constraints. The PCM is also responsible for distributing the current, updated scheduling information to all users and resources that utilize it daily. This is referred to as *Centralized Scheduling*. Depending on the size of the organization, there may be a need for multiple PCM's to manage individual segment schedules of the entire workflow system. Each schedule should be built so it can tie into the overall Master Schedule to assure all critical path tasks of the system are completed on schedule. The PCM or one of the PMCs should be designated to manage the Master Schedule.

The need for correct communication regarding schedules is at the core of creating operational

---

[5] Primavera is project management software by the Oracle Corporation.

excellence. Regardless of whether internal or external team members use the information, the information must always be accurate and up-to-date. Nothing builds confidence in the schedule(s) and the organization faster than providing real-time, accurate information. As I have stated, every function within the organization should have a schedule that is a sub-schedule of the Master Schedule. In the homebuilding industry, one of the most critical schedules concerns the production of new houses. I will use the production schedule of new homes as an example to illustrate my points, but any type of schedule is similar.

First, I want to share another real-life story of inaccurate schedule information costing real money. Upon my arrival at one homebuilding organization, one of the major suppliers of building materials was so accustomed to receiving inaccurate scheduling information that they had a full-time employee dedicated to driving around to ensure that our job sites were ready for deliveries and installation. There was absolutely zero trust in the schedule. Believe me, we were paying for that employee and all the dry run deliveries that the supplier and other trade contractors were experiencing. This situation, alone and among many others, can quickly add up to real wasted dollars. This example is not about operational excellence, but rather about saving wasted money by communicating accurate scheduling information.

We embarked on a mission to quickly gain trust in the production schedule from everyone who relied on the schedule information. We did not change the existing schedule in any way to begin with, and there was *A LOT* of room for improvement. We wanted to build trust that the current schedule was being communicated accurately. Remember, we need to crawl before we walk, and so on. We ensured that a process was in place to automatically transmit a two-week outlook of updated scheduling information daily to all relevant parties. Then we told everyone who relied on the schedule information of our plan to improve the schedule process and build their trust in the schedule information. We communicated to everyone responsible for updating the production schedule daily that complete accuracy was a requirement and nothing less was expected. We also communicated that it was acceptable to record delays and variances, regardless of whether they were caused by us or someone else. We just needed complete truth and accuracy, no matter what the circumstance. The ultimate objective was never to have to make a scheduling phone call and rely solely on the daily transmitted electronic schedule, unless there was a last-minute variance that required immediate communication.

One of the first things we did was to implement the *5-1 Ready* call process. This process was only done temporarily to confirm to the resource(s) that what they were seeing on their daily electronic copy of their schedule was correct. We required the Production Manager or Superintendent responsible for maintaining and updating the production schedule for their managed homes to make contact (by phone) with the upcoming scheduled resource(s). The first contact was made five days before when the resource was expected to start their task on the specific construction project. The reason for the 5-day contact point was that most of the resources requested a 5-day lead time (advance notice). The second contact was made with the scheduled resource one day before they were expected to begin work, to ensure their schedule compliance and that the construction project was ready for them to start work as scheduled. The 5-1 Ready process was implemented for a short period to build confidence in the production schedule information.

The second key component to building trust in the electronic schedule was *inspecting what was expected*. In other words, the management team would make random field inspections of the houses under construction to confirm that the daily submitted electronic schedule reflected the actual results in the field. If the schedule were accurate, we would praise the Construction Manager responsible. If the results were inaccurate, we would stress again to the responsible Construction Manager the importance of having accurate updates. We would also speak with them about the consequences of ongoing noncompliance. After a short time, we had gained confidence in the daily published schedule and the 5-1 Ready process, and the random field inspections were no longer needed.

I have already discussed building all schedules using CPM; now, let me address a few additional points that are necessary for creating a proper schedule.

- Define all the tasks, including inspections and material releases (deliveries).
- Place the tasks in order of dependency.
- Define the duration of each task. (I recommend using a per-hour or per-day duration.)
- Identify the current and necessary capacity of each task.
- Resource lead time should be determined on a case-by-case basis.
- Identify the critical path of the schedule.
- Identify the Start and Finish (early and late) dates of each task.

Once the schedule is completed and the critical path of the schedule is defined, you can determine which noncritical tasks have *Float Days* (Buffer Time) and how many float days each task has. A task with float days should never be a constrained task.

Now, I would like to discuss ways to reduce the schedule's overall duration (Cycle Time Reduction) and make it more efficient and profitable. I discussed earlier that we did not make any changes to the existing production schedule while we were in the process of gaining confidence in the automated schedule information. Additionally, I mentioned earlier the concept of 'crawling before you walk,' and so on. Several aspects of the current production schedule required significant improvements. One example was that the current production schedule was engineered using a six-month overall duration. Still, we were completing the construction of the houses in an average of nine months. There were numerous extremely costly delays. But I am a firm believer that you need irrefutable evidence (data) to convince someone they need to and can make improvements. The resistance to change is stiff to overcome, just because you say it needs to change. You need accurate data. One thing we noticed very quickly through our daily updated scheduling data was that many resources were not meeting their initial scheduled start date. Still, they were completing the task on the expected finish date. The resources and the construction managers both thought that the schedule was not being delayed, so everything was proceeding as planned. However, the information indicated that the resources had too much slack time in their task duration to make up for their delayed starts. With the newly gained information, we instituted a new scheduling rule that was communicated to every construction manager and every resource, regardless of their job task. *The rule consisted of every resource being required to start their work on the first day of their scheduled task with a whole crew and remain on the job every day until the*

work was completed to the expected quality. I felt that the new rule was more than reasonable and not asking too much of the resources, since we were providing them with a daily updated two-week schedule outlook, and most of them requested only a five-day notice. This new rule had a profoundly positive impact on reducing the overall duration of the schedule, enabling immediate improvements in cycle time. We communicated that we would track the number of delay days for each resource and the reason for each delay. Earlier, we had discussed with everyone the negative financial impact that even just one day of delayed throughput would produce. The business owners who were part of the external resources realized all the ramifications a single day delay attributable to their organization would bring. Additionally, the owners were entrepreneurs who recognized that once their resources had been allocated and the work commenced, it was more profitable for their organization to complete the task as quickly as possible. Hence, since the new rule was implemented, no resource wanted delays attributed to them, and the scheduling data clearly showed that the current task durations were too long. With the new rule firmly in place and the scheduling information credible, it was easy to convince the resources and the construction managers that the time durations of most tasks were unnecessarily too long. We gradually decreased the task durations incrementally. Leaving enough task duration that would give the resources a comfort level that they still could complete the task on schedule. We continued to collect schedule data and, in a short time, worked on getting every task to the proper duration. The schedule data and accountability for the data now enable us to make substantial improvements in reducing delays and shortening the duration of many tasks. Also, the quality of the work improved. Each resource knew that their work needed to be 100% complete with excellent quality, the first time, so that schedule delays would not be attributed to them. Every resource became an additional quality control manager. We communicated that every resource was required to *Pull the Chord* if any defect was discovered in the preceding work. This allowed for any known defect to be addressed immediately. We also held the resources accountable for covering up bad work. The original resource that created the defect was held accountable, along with the resource responsible for covering the defective work. Whoever said speed sacrifices quality was mistaken and did not understand how to create a proper production process. By increasing our focus on every area of the production schedule and continuing to communicate to everyone that total accuracy and compliance with all schedules were a requirement, the production schedule was reduced to a total of five months, and the average build time decreased from nine months to slightly over five months. Thus, decreasing cycle time and increasing inventory turns. Cycle time reduction has multiple benefits, but ultimately, the implementation of this one rule increased throughput, which significantly improved net profitability. Time is truly money.

But we were not finished improving the schedule. The target was to reduce the overall duration of the production schedule to four months and eliminate all delays. The increased monitoring of the schedule by everyone involved continued to minimize delays, and the average build time moved much closer to the current schedule template of five months. As we continued to work toward completing each new home within the five-month schedule template's time frame, we collaborated with each resource to identify schedule duration improvements. We were seeking additional creative ways to reduce the schedule duration. One approach discussed was to schedule the HVAC, plumbing, and electrical rough-in tasks to be completed simultaneously in the house. This was a new way of thinking because, historically, each trade contractor had wanted to conduct their work while being alone in the house. We discussed this possibility with each resource that would be affected by the rough-in tasks. They were all reluctant to try the new idea to begin with, but we explained that there were three separate trades and three separate floors. Most of our home designs had three floors: a basement, main floor, and second floor. It was suggested that they could each begin their work on a different floor and trade places on the floors to avoid overlapping work. We also reminded the contractors that if we continued to reduce the duration of the production schedule, we could increase the inventory turns, resulting in more houses being built annually, more work, and higher annual profitability for them. We all decided to implement this in a few houses on a trial basis. We did not just cram this change down their throats. We all came together as a team to discuss the pros and cons of the idea, and we collectively decided to give it a try. It did not take too many houses for the contractors to realize that the new scheduling process worked better for them than before. They loved it. The main benefit to them was that they could discuss with each other in real-time, where each contractor planned to locate their specific work and work through any conflicts, instead of having to return to the jobsite at a later date for rework. By incorporating the new enhancement into the schedule template, we were able to significantly reduce the overall duration. We continued to explore ways to reduce the schedule's overall duration, generating additional ideas to further optimize it. Your system may be different, but if you think creatively, you will find additional ways to improve each of your schedules. This is referred to as *Ongoing Continuous Improvement*.

Another area of improvement (there are many others) I want to touch on requires a shift in old, incorrect thinking. I discussed in a previous chapter the need to move away from cost accounting and towards throughput accounting. I will use this example to illustrate my point. The idea of implementing pre-fabricated panelized wall and floor systems were considered to reduce the duration of the schedule further. The pros and cons of this new idea were analyzed, and it was discovered that the revised cost of the prefabricated panel installation by the framers did not fully offset the new cost of pre-building the panelized components off-site. Even though implementing this new panelized process would make a substantial reduction in the production schedule duration. There was stiff resistance from the Purchasing Team because the **cost** of the completed task increased the original budget slightly. The team members of the purchasing department had been programmed to reduce all costs and not allow any increase. They were stuck in the obsolete cost accounting mindset. Their thinking was incorrect. They needed to shift their thinking to *Throughput Accounting*. They were going to waste huge dollars on increased throughput while saving pennies on decreased costs. Again, I had to use irrefutable data to convince them that implementing this schedule improvement process would result in a positive increase in annual throughput revenue, which would far outweigh the additional costs incurred by the production budget.

You need to control each task's duration and capacity as much as possible. Consider everything you can control and improve in the process. Then think about steps in the process that would typically be considered out of your control. Think out of the ordinary. If you believe it cannot be accomplished, you are already defeated. Do not think negatively. Remember, you can do **all** things through Christ, who gives you strength. He has given you everything you need to accomplish His plan for your life, which includes being excellent. You need to trust and rely on Him to provide you with the creative ideas to continue to improve. You need to ask Him to direct your steps and give you His favor and wisdom. Then listen for His prompting. Be a positive thinker. You will never know what can be achieved unless you go after it. If it doesn't go as planned the first time, don't give up. Learn from your experience, make the necessary adjustments, and pursue it again. If you can see it in your mind and genuinely believe it can be done, then you will see it in your life.

A good example of a situation in homebuilding that is typically considered beyond your control is that of jurisdictional building inspections. Just like every task in a schedule, a process needs to be established that allows the task to be executed with the highest efficiency. Start by showing the building department official how implementing a more efficient schedule process will benefit them. Show them how proper schedule management will decrease the overall duration of the schedule while increasing inventory turns. This will enable more homes to be built each year, resulting in increased annual revenue from additional building permits and impact fees. Increased revenue (money) always talks. Explain to the Chief Building Official the plan to decrease the schedule duration and

ask for their feedback on their ideas to improve their segment of the schedule process. It is always better to implement a jointly derived improved process than to demand improvement. Your objective is to work with each jurisdiction to develop precise inspection and re-inspection processes that will enable you to calculate the schedule duration more accurately. You want to eliminate the unknowns and potential delays as much as possible. You must think of unique ways to make every possible reduction in the overall schedule duration.

At this point, I need to discuss additional responsibilities of the Process Control Manager as they relate to schedule and resource management. If the system has more than one assembly line that runs concurrently and uses the same resources, this information is crucial. As I stated earlier, the PCM should be solely responsible for resource management when it comes to allocating additional capacity or deficient capacity if the schedule is not being followed precisely. The PCM can observe each assembly line and best determine how to manage resources effectively. The production manager of each assembly line is unaware of what is happening on other assembly lines or in different areas within the system. Also, each resource should not be allowed to manage the schedule in any way. They must follow the schedule exactly. If the resource is meeting the daily schedule of each assembly line and wants to provide additional excess capacity, it **MUST** be allocated by the PCM. Suppose additional capacity is allowed and assigned by the PCM. In that case, the impacted production manager must give the following downstream resource the *option* to move up their schedule or wait for the original schedule date. This usually occurs within the downline resource's lead time, and they must not be forced to move up their schedule. When deviations from the schedule occur, they must be approved by the PCM.

For example, suppose a resource has extra capacity and calls their favorite production manager in isolation without consulting the PCM. In that case, the extra capacity may not be utilized in the most effective way for the system. Instruct the PCM to allocate any additional capacity to the product that is most delayed at the time. Next, prioritize any contracted products that are delayed. The PCM should spend quality time with each resource to learn about their business processes and establish a strong, partner-like relationship built on trust. The PCM should assist each resource in understanding the principles contained in this book and help make their organizations more productive and profitable.

Some delays in the schedule are inevitable. Murphy's Law, which states: "Anything that can go wrong will go wrong," is still alive and well. Some things cannot be predicted with exact certainty. Some tasks have a time range that cannot be determined precisely, so account for the unexpected as much as possible.

One way to reduce delays is to maintain a reserve capacity. What I mean by reserve capacity is to establish primary and secondary resources for every task in the schedule. Think about a sports team. It has a first string and a second string. If the first-string player is unable to perform or is not performing to the expected standard, the coach substitutes the first-string player with the second-string player. Examine other industries and learn from their operational successes. Do not let your thinking become narrow-minded. In production homebuilding, there is typically more than one community (or assembly line) building new houses simultaneously. Include verbiage in the resource contract that establishes a primary resource for a specific community and a secondary backup resource. Make the primary resource on one assembly line the secondary resource on another assembly line, and vice versa. This way, each resource can be guaranteed a certain number of starts (houses to be built) allocated to them. Communicate and contract with every resource, so that if they are the primary resource and cannot adhere to the schedule in any way, the secondary resource will be called to complete the task. Some additional details need to be addressed with the resources that have multiple functions on the assembly line, such as the plumber, electrician, and HVAC technician. **This type of scenario assures a much better adherence to the schedule because the primary resource will make every effort not to lose work to the secondary resource.** Inform the primary resource if they miss their scheduled start date, that they are delaying the schedule, and the secondary resource will be called in. This may not delay the overall completion date of the schedule, as the time may be made up; however, they do not know that. They are delaying the schedule at that point. The statement "You are delaying the schedule" usually has extremely positive results. Again, the resources do not want any delays to be recorded against them because they have learned the extreme unnecessary costs and negative ramifications delays produce. Let me give you another actual example. We were on a community inspection at one particular house discussing proper schedule adherence with one of the Production Managers. The scheduled resource had informed the Production Manager earlier in the day that they would not be able to start their work as scheduled. As a teaching opportunity, we instructed the Production Manager to immediately call the resource and notify them that they were delaying the schedule. The delay would be recorded and attributed to their company. Also, the secondary resource would be called in if necessary. The call was made to the resource, and the Production Manager notified them of the situation and the ramifications. While still on the phone, the resource said, "Hold on, let me see what I can do". In a very short time, the resource came back on the phone to tell that a whole crew would be there within the hour to start the work. Holding the resource accountable to what they had agreed upon was all it took, but having communicated and documented processes allowed the Production Manager to address the resource confidently.

Keep in mind that as delays accumulate in a schedule, there is a possibility that later tasks will become constrained activities. The tasks downstream will require additional capacity to compensate for the prior delays and maintain the original desired schedules and throughput.

Another benefit of having a strong and reliable production scheduling process is the ability to make automatic electronic payments to the resources. Once the Production Manager confirms that a particular task has been completed adequately according to the daily schedule, the resource can be scheduled for automatic electronic payment. Remember, the Production Manager does not show the task completed on the schedule update until the task is 100% complete with the proper quality. This assures the resource is not paid too soon, and the adequate leverage is not lost. The terms of when the resource is to be paid after completion of the task should be outlined in the resource agreement.[6] Payment terms should be

---

[6] The resource agreement (Contractor Agreement) is outlined in detail in the chapter entitled Product Development and Purchasing.

determined on a case-by-case basis. However, in each case, the terms should be negotiated as far in advance as reasonably possible. Depending on the size of your organization and the amount of production, the resource could be paid virtually daily. Use the fact that they will be paid more often in the payment terms negotiations. Additionally, this enables the Accounts Payable department to operate on more precise, even flow principles.

Once the organization becomes operationally strong, total confidence in all processes is achieved, and customers rave about the product and service. Another extremely significant benefit of operational excellence that can be initiated is what is termed *Zero-Based Working Capital.* Combining automatic electronic payments with extended resource payment terms allows for minimum, if any, need for expensive operating capital. By being recognized in the marketplace as one of the best organizations to deal with, customers are more willing to accept the processes by which the organization conducts its business, even though they may differ from those of the competition. As the overall duration of the production schedules is reduced to three or even two months (which can and has been done), there is an opportunity to pay the majority of the production cost after the product has been completed, delivered, and all proceeds from the sale have been received. Let's say that ten percent of the product's sales price is required as a deposit from the customer before production begins. This initial deposit can be paid in multiple installments. However, using the customer deposit to cover the necessary initial product costs and extending the payment terms beyond the product delivery date can limit or eliminate the need for working capital. For example, in homebuilding, the combined price of framing materials and labor typically constitutes the most significant single expense. This task occurs approximately a quarter of the way through the house-building project. If you make the payment terms sixty days from completion, it will be beyond the product delivery and closing date. This should be easily negotiated with the resources, as the industry standard is already payment within thirty to forty-five days. Additionally, since the resources are to be paid automatically by electronic payment, recipients will receive payment on a weekly, if not daily, basis.

Effective time management yields excellent profitability.

Chapter 13

Product Development and Purchasing

To ensure that unexpected cost overruns and schedule delays continue to decrease, it is essential to develop firm, concise production plans, specifications, and scopes of work, as well as contracts and agreements, to communicate your expectations clearly. It is unfair, bad business, and, quite frankly, dishonest to provide any resource with inaccurate, incomplete, or conflicting documentation, then hold them solely responsible for performing their work accurately. When resources use inaccurate documents, their bids for work and the performance of their work will become unnecessarily costly in more ways than just wasted time and money. I am convinced that a significant amount of the work needs to be accurately completed before production can even begin. All documentation and expectations must be detailed and communicated for the entire workflow system. Communicate to every resource, both internal and external, the expectation that if any defect is identified in any area of the workflow process, including all documentation, it must be corrected immediately.

With the same organization I used as an example with production scheduling, there was also a need for improvements in Product Development processes and Purchasing processes.

In product development, one of the first steps we took was to create a schedule for developing a new product. Every function of the organization should follow a clearly defined schedule, for which they are held accountable for executing correctly. Like the production schedule, the product development schedule included milestone decision tasks that were required to be completed on time to keep the new product design on schedule. We also implemented a weekly *Product Design Meeting* similar to the Weekly Starts Meeting I described earlier. During this weekly meeting, we will review the new product schedule and address any concerns regarding project scheduling. We did not have meetings to have meetings. Each meeting had a specific agenda, and if there were no issues to discuss, the meeting would be over. Everything needs to be done PRODUCTIVELY. Another task we implemented in the schedule was that once the new or updated design entered the later stages of the Design Development Phase, it would undergo *Value and Structural Engineering.* Before the design was allowed to enter the final Construction Document Phase, the engineering process would begin by electronically sending the Design Development plan to the structural engineer, along with key resources such as the framer, plumber, electrician, HVAC specialist, and truss manufacturer. We also distributed the plan to our senior production staff and our purchasing staff for their review. We gave them each seventy-two hours to review the plan and note any necessary revisions or clarifications based on both structural and cost implications. We would then all meet together, including the architectural team, to discuss and implement each needed revision. By going through this process, we were able to produce a much more accurate and cost-effective set of production plans. Along with this process, the architecture team and the purchasing team were able to work together to produce more complete and accurate plan specifications and material takeoffs. Additionally, by going through this process, we were able to significantly reduce the extremely costly delays once the product began on the assembly line.

Another process that was implemented was the *Prototype Process.* The prototype process was developed to construct the new product in the field before it was utilized in ongoing production. This process allowed for the addressing of any additional deficient production items, whether in the plan documentation or the product itself. The prototype process was included as a sub-schedule within the new product design schedule. The prototype followed the same accelerated schedule as the designated model homes. The implementation of the value engineering process and the prototype process had a drastic, positive effect on the reduction of both costly (variances) schedule delays and budget overruns.

The *Plan Addenda* process was also introduced. This process was developed to create a structured approach for addressing any identified defects or needed revisions in a plan that had already been released for use in ongoing production. When a required plan update or clarification was identified, a detailed rough sketch of the necessary plan change would be forwarded to the architecture team. Once the architecture was completed, the change was returned to the appropriate production manager for design approval. After obtaining authorization, the architecture team would assign a designation number to the new plan addenda, update the design in the master plan for the affected product, and create the plan addenda accordingly. Then, the architecture would forward the plan addenda to purchasing. Pricing updates, if any, would be obtained from each resource affected by the plan addenda. Updated Purchase Orders would be distributed to each resource affected, along with complete documentation of the newly created plan addenda. Additionally, the new addenda would be sent to the Sales Department, and every production manager responsible for building the specific product affected by the plan would be informed. As a rule, after a plan had accumulated ten addenda, the master plan would be updated and given a new release date.

The Purchasing functions also needed significant improvements. Without exception, every production dollar spent by the organization **MUST** be covered by a

Purchase Order or a *Variance Purchase Order*. If the organization does not have a current purchase order system, implementing one is vital to achieving operational excellence and should be done immediately. The Purchase Order process is absolutely a required fundamental of any successful purchasing and accounting function. Each expense must be accounted for up front. It is much easier to negotiate prices, maintain accurate material packs, and so on when the Purchase Order (P.O.) or Variance Purchase Order (V.P.O.) is executed and completed before any work begins. **I cannot stress this enough**. Each team member, both internal and external, needs to understand that NO WORK is to be started without a pre-approved Purchase Order or Variance Purchase Order. Every resource should realize that if any work is started without a P.O. or V.P.O., they do so at their own risk of not getting paid. This is another effective way to ensure that defects are identified. A Purchase Order is a resource authorization to execute the work. Without a P.O. system, how can budget compliance be adequately monitored? And, without strict compliance with V.P.O. rules, how can unbudgeted expenses be effectively managed and accounted for? Knowing the expected costs before production begins is essential.

As I stated at the beginning of this chapter, it is imperative, for multiple reasons, that all of the organization's documentations and communications are clear and precise. As we were working on implementing and improving product design documentation processes we were also working on the purchasing documentation processes. After talking with the resources and the production managers, it quickly became apparent that the current Scopes of Work were inadequate. Most were incomplete, or in a few cases, there were no Scopes of Work at all. The lack of accurate Scopes of Work was confusing many, incomplete budgets, V.P.O.s, and cost overruns. Therefore, we, as a team, embarked on reviewing and updating all Scopes of Work. We would meet on Saturday mornings for four hours with a select group of key individuals from the production, purchasing, and architectural teams. Each week, we would invite the resources that were impacted by the scopes we were dealing with that day. The organization would provide lunch as an incentive for attendance and to express gratitude for participants giving up part of their weekend. Much more quickly than expected, we had gone through and accurately updated each Scope of Work. We continued to track the reasons for V.P.O.'s, and occasionally, we would identify a Scope of Work that needed further updates. Again, by properly addressing the incomplete Scopes of Work, we were able to significantly reduce the heartache for many and increase the profits for the organization and the resources. This is another benefit of operational excellence.

The following item that needed to be addressed and improved was contract documentation. Detailed and accurate Scopes of Work, along with correct Contracts, virtually clarified every aspect of what was expected of each resource. By having concise information and expectations, we were able to keep *The High Ground* when resources fell short of the contracted terms. What I mean by the high ground is that when every contract document, such as the production plans, scopes of work, specifications, contracts, and purchase orders, is accurate and concise, it is much easier to hold a resource accountable to the agreed-upon terms. I use the phrase *"help me understand."* When all the documentation provided to a resource is entirely accurate and complete, it is easy to say, "Help me understand why you are not following our agreement when it is written here in black and white." Significant leverage is maintained, and the relationship does not suffer because it allows you to keep the high ground, and the resource cannot dispute that the documentation is correct. If, or when, a V.P.O. is written due to inaccurate documentation, this is a clear indication that additional improvement is needed.

Let us address Resource Contracts. In most Resource Contracts, there are a few specific topics that should be included and agreed upon in every resource contract. I have listed the major issues.

Proven Principles and Methodologies to Achieve Increased Profitability

- General Conditions and Scope of Work
- Contract Pricing and Payment Terms
- Change or Addition to Work or Materials
- Time
- Clean Up
- Taxes and Permits
- Insurance and Indemnity
- Liquidated Damages
- Warranty
- Safety Practices and Hazardous Materials
- Recourse by Builder
- Arbitration of Disputes
- Attorney Fee
- Exhibits
- Miscellaneous
- Entire Agreement
- Acceptance

Have the resource contract worded in such a way that if the primary resource is unable to meet the schedule, the secondary resource can and will be used. Include the requirement of the *Request for Bid Sheet* being broken down by *Unit-Based Pricing*. Maintain yearly pricing-type contracts, if possible. Get the best terms, pricing, longest payment terms, and best activity durations. Additionally, when contracting, keep in mind that even flow principles should be applied consistently throughout the workflow system. Traditionally, in homebuilding, Re-contracting takes place in November or December of each year or later months of the fiscal year. **This is not using even flow**. Re-contracting should be done continually throughout the year based on even flow principles by having at least yearly contract renewal terms. One reason this is done is to prevent the purchasing team from being rushed to complete all re-contracting within a short time frame. This enables accurate and comprehensive contracting. Set up the contracts with all resources concisely based on the workflow processes and the desired outcome. I have included several pages in the following document, which is an example of a homebuilding resource agreement that I have put together and successfully used for many years.

CONTRACTOR AGREEMENT

THIS AGREEMENT, made as of (Current Date), in the Year of (Current Year),

Between the Builder:	**Builder Full Name** **Builder Primary Full Address** **Builder Telephone** **Builder Email Address**
And the Contractor:	**Contractor Full Name** **Contractor Primary Full Address** **Contractor Telephone** **Contractor Email Address**
For the Project:	**Project Description** **Plan Description**

ARTICLE 1.   GENERAL CONDITIONS AND SCOPE OF WORK (EXHIBIT "A")

1.1. The Agreement applies to the Project described above (hereinafter "Project(s)") for which the Contractor hereinafter provides Work to the Builder. The term "Project(s)" includes the lot or land on which construction is occurring. The Agreement applies to both Projects being constructed on land owned by another and to Projects being built on land owned by the Builder. The term "Construction Manager" refers to the person acting as the agent of the Builder to direct all construction activities of the Project.

1.2. The Contractor is presumed to have reviewed and compared the drawings, specifications, and the scope of work covered by this Agreement and to have reported any discrepancies to the Construction Manager in writing. He should visit the site to verify locations of existing facilities and report to the Builder and Construction Manager any site conditions that will adversely affect the work. Contractor is to provide all work, materials, labor, and equipment in full accordance with the latest rules and regulations of the Uniform Building Codes, all City and County Codes and Regulations, and other applicable laws or regulations, and shall perform all work in a good workmanlike manner. Nothing in these Plans or Specifications is to be construed to permit work not conforming to all prevailing codes. The Contractor agrees to remedy or repair all work not accepted by the City or County, which has jurisdictional authority over the project, at no additional expense to the Builder.

1.3. Contractor has heretofore entered into a contract with said Builder to furnish all **_labor, material, equipment, and supervision_** necessary to perform all work described below according to the construction documents. Note: Labor and Materials not explicitly defined, which are incidental to the installation, without which a satisfactory operating system or finished product cannot be reasonably completed, are part of the work. *CONTRACTOR AGREES TO COMPLETE THE WORK IN A WORKMANLIKE MANNER, FREE FROM ANY AND ALL DEFECTS.*

1.4. The Plans, the Specifications (Exhibit C), the Scope of Work (Exhibit A), along with the Contractor's Bid Sheet (Exhibit B) together with any written and signed supplements or modifications thereto for the project, are incorporated into the Agreement, and shall hereinafter be referred to collectively as the "Work".

1.5. General Responsibilities: In addition to its other responsibilities under this Agreement, Contractor shall have the following responsibilities:

   a. Contractor shall procure and pay for all permits, licenses, and inspections required by any governmental authority for any part of the Work and shall furnish any bonds, security, or deposits required by such authority to permit performance of the Work.

   b. Contractor shall comply with, and ensure the compliance by its employees, subcontractors, and agents with all applicable federal, state, and local laws, ordinances, statutes, rules, and regulations, including those relating to wages, hours, fair employment practices, nondiscrimination, immigration and naturalization, occupational safety or health, and working conditions. The safety of the Contractor's employees, subcontractors, and agents, whether or not in common work areas, is the responsibility of the Contractor. Exercise of proper safety procedures is considered to be an integral part of this Work.

c. Contractor shall coordinate the installation of the Work with other interfacing trades courteously and professionally, so as not to interfere with them, delay them, or damage their work.

d. Contractor shall conduct the Work to avoid causing damage to any part of the Project. Contractor shall be responsible for all such damage.

e. Contractor shall provide a qualified onsite supervisor/foreman whenever the Work is being performed.

f. Contractor shall not remove or damage silt fencing or other erosion control devices.

g. Contractor shall keep all vehicles off Projects, including driveways, unless expressly permitted by the Construction Manager to drive onto a Project for a limited purpose.

h. Contractor shall not use or permit the use by any of its employees, subcontractors, suppliers, or agents of alcoholic beverages or controlled substances on or in connection with the Project or the Work.

i. Contractor shall not cover any known defect in the Work or work by someone else but shall immediately notify Construction Manager of such defect and obtain permission in writing to continue the pertinent aspect of the Work. If Contractor covers defective work performed by Contractor or the defective work of someone else, the Contractor agrees to pay the costs to uncover and repair the defective work.

j. Contractor shall not allow food or smoking inside the Project at any time.

k. The Contractor shall not allow shoes to be worn, or if worn, they must be adequately covered inside a Project with finished flooring installed.

l. Contractor shall not permit profanity, loud conversations or music, or any other behavior likely to disturb others working on a Project or persons living in proximity to a Project.

m. Contractor understands that it is not authorized to discuss or adjust prices with anyone. Any such requests should be referred to the Construction Manager.

n. Contractor shall limit its interactions with any third parties to avoid confusion between Builder, or Construction Manager, and these persons, and shall refer questions from them to Construction Manager. Contractor shall not offer them advice or opinions.

o. Contractor shall immediately inform Builder and Construction Manager of any change of its address or telephone numbers set forth above.

p. Contractor is fully responsible, in contract and tort, for the performance of the Work that it subcontracts to anyone else.

q. Contractor shall effectually secure and protect the Work done hereunder and assume full responsibility for the condition thereof until final acceptance by the Building Official having jurisdiction over the project, Construction Manager, and Builder. The Contractor further agrees to provide such protection as is necessary to safeguard the Work and the workmen of the Builder and other contractors from the effects of their operations. Contractor shall be liable for any loss or damage to any work in place or to any equipment and materials on the project site caused by him or his agents, employees, or guests.

ARTICLE 2. CONTRACT PRICING AND PAYMENT TERMS

2.1. Contractor understands and agrees that progress payment requests shall be written in the form of a Purchase Order (P.O.) or Variance Purchase Order (V.P.O.) and given to the Builder. **All work for the requested portion must be completed before payment is made.** Once the work is fully completed and approved by the Builder, an automatic electronic payment will be made in **(Calendar Days)** to the bank account number specified below. **(Bank Routing and Account Numbers).** Please note that a certificate of Workman's Compensation Insurance and all other insurance required must be received and remain in effect before any payment is made, or the Builder will hold total payment or may choose to withhold a percentage needed to cover the labor portion of the work. As a condition precedent to any payment, or otherwise upon demand, Builder will require Contractor to provide partial or complete (as appropriate) lien releases. It is agreed that no payment hereunder shall be made, except at the Builder's option, until and unless such documents have been furnished as permitted by **(State Name)** law.

2.2. The Total Contract Amount for the work outlined in this agreement shall be: **Per Start Release** $_____(subject to additions and deletions for changes made according to the provisions of this agreement). The Contractor's Bid Sheet shall list all individual unit prices for material, labor, and equipment.

2.3. The Contract Price and all terms of this agreement are in effect from the signing date of this agreement and continue for Twelve Months (subject to price modifications according to the provisions of this agreement).

2.4. Contractor understands and agrees that the Total Contract Amount covered under the terms of this agreement remains in effect for the entire construction time as long as the actual start date of the first scheduled activity of the specific project and/or the issuance of a Purchase Order to the Contractor is on or before the expiration date of this agreement.

2.5. Contractor's submission of a Purchase Order (P.O.) or Variance Purchase Order (V.P.O.) to be paid shall constitute a warranty and representation by Contractor to Builder that Contractor has performed that portion of the Work covered by the P.O. or V.P.O. in full compliance with this Agreement, and has paid for all labor, materials, supplies, equipment, tools and other items used in performance of the Work. It has obtained legally binding partial or final lien waivers from all such persons or entities. The Builder may require proof of such payment and waivers before making payments to the Contractor.

2.6. BACKCHARGES: Notwithstanding any other provisions in this Agreement, Builder, without prejudice to any other rights or remedies under this Agreement may at its election, back charge Contractor for costs, expenses, losses, liabilities and all other damages which Builder sustains as a result of acts, omissions or breaches by Contractor including by example but not limitation, delays, failure to clean up and failure to perform warranty work. Builder and/or Construction Manager shall prepare a Back Charge Work Up Sheet, which will set forth the work to be performed (if any), price, and reason for the back charge, and shall deliver a copy thereof to the Contractor. Back charges may be deducted from progress or final payments.

ARTICLE 3.   CHANGE OR ADDITIONS TO WORK OR MATERIALS

3.1. Builder reserves the right to order work changes like additions, deletions, or modifications without invalidating the Agreement, and Contractor agrees to make all changes, furnish the materials, and perform the work which Builder may require.

3.2. Contractor understands and agrees that no change orders or contract additions will be made unless agreed to in writing by Builder and Construction Manager. If any additional work is performed and not covered by this contract, the Contractor shall proceed at their own risk and expense. The Contractor understands that it is not authorized to make changes to the Work at the request of a third party without obtaining written direction from both the Builder and the Construction Manager, as per the Agreement. Any requests for changes should be referred to the Construction Manager. No alterations, additions, or minor changes can be made to the work or method of performance without a written change order signed by the Builder, Construction Manager, and Contractor.

3.3. Should extra work outside of this Agreement be required for unforeseen conditions, Contractor shall perform additional work on a time and material basis with material at cost plus fifteen percent (15%) and labor at the following rate:

(Laborer) $_____ / hour

(Foreman) $_____ / hour

ARTICLE 4. TIME

4.1. Time is of the essence in this Agreement. The Construction Manager shall provide the Contractor with scheduling information and a proposed schedule for the performance of his work. Contractor shall conform to the Construction Manager's progress schedule and all revisions or changes made thereto. Within **(number of days)** after being notified by the Construction Manager of the Project schedule, Contractor shall commence actual construction of the Work and shall thereafter diligently continue the Work to completion. Contractor shall coordinate the work covered by this Agreement with that of all other contractors, subcontractors, and of Builder, in a manner that will facilitate the efficient completion of the entire work. In the event Contractor fails to maintain his part of Construction Manager's schedule, he shall, without additional compensation, accelerate the work as Construction Manager may direct until Contractor's work is per such schedule.

4.2. Contractor shall keep both an adequate size and a professionally trained crew on the job site each day to complete the Contractor's portion of the project within **(number of days)** and work within the project schedule.

4.3. Contractor shall prepare and obtain approval as required by the Contract Documents for all shop drawings, details, samples, and do all other things necessary and incidental to the prosecution of his work in conformance with the Construction Manager's progress schedule.

4.4. Damages caused by delays: If Contractor should default in performance of the work described in this Agreement, or should otherwise commit any act which causes delay to the original completion of the prime contract work, Contractor shall be liable for all losses, costs, expenses, liabilities, and damages sustained by Builder. As a minimum and without prejudice to any other remedies herein, Contractor agrees to pay Builder the sum of **two hundred fifty dollars ($250.00)** for each day of delay.

4.5. Inspection Failures: If Contractor should fail governmental inspections of the work described in this Agreement, Contractor, without prejudice to any other remedies afforded Builder herein, shall be liable for the following deductions from the Contract Price:

Inspection Failure	Deduction
1st	None
2nd	0.01% of the Contract Price but not less than $300.00
3rd	0.5% of the Contract Price but not less than $1,000.00
4th	1.0% of the Contract Price but not less than $2,000.00

In no event, however, shall an inspection failure apply to the first of each building type subject to governmental inspections.

ARTICLE 5.   CLEAN-UP

5.1. The Contractor will be responsible for cleaning up the jobsite daily, including all generated construction debris, empty drink cans, food wrappers, and other trash. The contractor is responsible for placing all trash and any construction debris created as a result of the Work in the area designated by the Construction Manager. General pathways are to remain clean at all times. Contractor agrees, upon terminating his work at the site, to conduct general cleanup operations, including all areas of the site affected by his work. If necessary, the Contractor will be back-charged for cleanup costs by deducting the appropriate amount from future payments. Any tangible personal property left on or about the premises after the work by Contractor, supplier, subcontractor, etc. will immediately become the property of Builder, and it may dispose of such property in any manner. It may charge the Contractor, supplier, subcontractor, etc., for such disposal.

ARTICLE 6.   TAXES AND PERMITS

6.1. Contractor is an independent contractor of Builder and is not an employee of Builder. The Contractor understands and agrees that he shall be responsible for all taxes, fees, and expenses imposed directly or indirectly for his work, labor, material, and services required by law to fulfill this contract. The Contractor is responsible for obtaining all necessary permits in accordance with applicable laws, ordinances, and regulations where the work is performed. *CONTRACTOR SHALL BE SOLELY RESPONSIBLE FOR WITHHOLDING TAXES, SOCIAL SECURITY TAXES, INCOME TAXES, AND UNEMPLOYMENT TAXES FOR ALL EMPLOYEES OF CONTRACTOR.*

ARTICLE 7.   INSURANCE AND INDEMNITY

7.1.   The Contractor shall maintain, at his own expense, complete insurance including: (a) workers compensation insurance; (b) general liability insurance; (c) property damage insurance; and (d) automotive public liability and automotive property damage insurance on its work until final approval of the work described in the contract and for the entire term of this Agreement. The limits and terms of such coverage shall be set forth on the Certificates of Insurance provided to the Builder before the execution of this Agreement. Each Certificate of Insurance shall name the Contractor as the certificate holder and shall state that the insurance will not be cancelled without thirty (30) days' written notice to the Builder. The certificate of general liability policy shall name the Builder as an additional insured. The Contractor shall not hold the Builder liable for all costs, damages, fees, and expenses from any claims arising on the project. Failure of the Contractor to maintain appropriate insurance coverage may deem a material breach, allowing the Builder to terminate this contract or to provide insurance at the Contractor's expense.

7.2. To the fullest extent permitted by law, the Contractor shall indemnify and hold harmless the Builder, Builder's representatives, agents and employees from all claims, losses, damages and expenses, including attorney's fees arising out of or resulting from the performance of the Work, or failure to adhere to all provisions of this Agreement provided that such claim, loss, damage or expense is caused in whole or in part by any negligent act or omission of the Contractor, anyone directly employed by them or anyone whose acts they are liable for, and attributes to bodily injury, sickness, disease or death, mold growth, or to injury to or destruction of tangible property (other than the work itself) including any resulting loss of use, regardless of whether or not it is caused in part by a party indemnified above.

ARTICLE 8.   LIQUIDATED DAMAGES

8.1. If the project work is not completed on the stated completion date, the Contractor shall pay to the Builder the sum of **two hundred fifty dollars ($250.00)** for each calendar day of inexcusable delay until the work is completed, as liquidated damages.

ARTICLE 9.   WARRANTY

9.1. Contractor represents and warrants the following for its materials and work, as well as the materials of others used in the scope of Contractor's work.

9.2. <u>Contractor Warranties.</u> The Contractor represents and warrants to Builder that all equipment and materials used in the work and made a part of the structures thereon or placed permanently in connection therewith will be new unless otherwise specified in the Contract Documents, of good quality, free from defects, and in conformity with the Contract Documents. It is understood between the parties hereto that all equipment and materials not so in conformity are defective. CONTRACTOR FURTHER WARRANTS AT CONTRACTOR'S EXPENSE ALL LABOR AND MATERIALS FURNISHED BY HIM TO BE FREE OF DEFECT FOR AT LEAST ONE (1) YEAR FROM THE DATE OF CERTIFICATE OF OCCUPANCY OR FROM THE DATE OF THE DEED CONVEYING THE PROPERTY TO THE ULTIMATE PURCHASER, WHICHEVER DATE IS LATEST. PLUMBING, ELECTRICAL, MECHANICAL, AND FRAMING CONTRACTORS HEREBY WARRANT AT CONTRACTOR'S EXPENSE, ALL LABOR AND MATERIAL FOR A SECOND YEAR AS SPECIFIED BY BUILDER. CONTRACTOR AGREES TO MAKE ALL REPAIRS AND CORRECT SUCH DEFECTS UNDER THE WARRANTY WITHIN EIGHT (8) HOURS OF NOTICE OF SUCH DEFECT IN AN EMERGENCY AND FORTY-EIGHT (48) HOURS OF NOTICE OF SUCH DEFECT ON A NON-EMERGENCY BASIS. BUILDER SHALL DETERMINE THE EMERGENCY. THE PARTIES UNDERSTAND AND AGREE THAT THE ABOVE WARRANTIES ARE IN ADDITION TO AND DO NOT LIMIT ANY AND ALL STATUTORY WARRANTIES AND OTHER REMEDIES AFFORDED THE OWNER/BUILDER UNDER THE LAWS OF THE **(State Name).** CONTRACTOR EXPRESSLY AGREES THAT ALL WARRANTIES MADE BY HIM IN THIS AGREEMENT SHALL SURVIVE THIS AGREEMENT IN THE EVENT IT IS TERMINATED OR EXPIRES <u>FOR ANY REASON</u> BEFORE THE RUNNING OF THE FULL WARRANTY PERIOD.

9.3. <u>Manufacturer's Warranties.</u> Contractor shall furnish all certificates required by the municipality and/or VA and/or FHA. Contractor shall also provide all warranties, guarantees, certifications, and any other written documentation to Builder from Manufacturers for appliances, equipment, and any other materials used by Contractor in the completion of the scope of work. If the Contractor fails to furnish the said warranties and/or guarantees, the Contractor shall be responsible for such warranties and guarantees, as well as all damages resulting therefrom. *CONTRACTOR WARRANTS THAT CONTRACTOR HAS REVIEWED ALL MANUFACTURER'S SPECIFICATIONS FOR INSTALLATION AND USE OF ANY AND ALL MATERIALS, EQUIPMENT, APPLIANCES, AND ANY AND ALL OTHER MATERIALS INSTALLED AND/OR USED BY CONTRACTOR AND CONTRACTOR WARRANTS THAT CONTRACTOR WILL INSTALL ALL MATERIALS AND EQUIPMENT PER MANUFACTURER'S SPECIFICATION. IN THE EVENT BUILDER REQUESTS ANY CHANGE ORDER WHICH WOULD CAUSE INSTALLATION TO VARY FROM AND/OR BE INCONSISTANT WITH MANUFACTURER'S SPECIFICATIONS, CONTRACTOR SHALL NOTIFY BUILDER AND CONSTRUCTION MANAGER, IN WRITING, OF SUCH VARIANCE AND UNLESS WRITTEN AUTHORIZATION AND RELEASE IS RECEIVED FROM BUILDER, CONTRACTOR SHALL BE RESPONSIBLE FOR ANY AND ALL DAMAGES RESULTING FROM ANY INSTALLATION WHICH VARIES FROM MANUFACTURER'S SPECIFICATIONS.*

ARTICLE 10.   SAFETY PRACTICES AND HAZARDOUS MATERIALS

10.1. Contractor shall comply fully with all laws, orders, citations, rules, regulations, standards, and statutes concerning occupational health and safety, the handling and storage of hazardous materials, accident prevention, safety equipment, and practices. Contractor shall conduct inspections to determine that safe working conditions and equipment exist and accepts sole responsibility for providing a safe place to work for its employees and employees of its subcontractors and suppliers of material and equipment, for adequacy of and required use of all safety equipment and full compliance with the aforesaid laws, orders, citations, rules, regulations, standards and statutes.

10.2. Both parties agree that dealing with hazardous materials, waste, or asbestos requires specialized training, processes, precautions, and licenses. Therefore, unless the scope of this agreement includes the specific handling, disturbance, removal, or transportation of hazardous materials, waste, or asbestos, upon discovery of such dangerous materials, the Contractor shall notify the Builder immediately and allow the Builder to contract with an appropriately licensed and qualified hazardous material contractor.

10.3. Should Contractor require the use of any hazardous materials on the jobsite, the Contractor shall first notify Builder and Construction Manager of its nature and obtain written permission to enter the jobsite. If said permission is obtained, Contractor shall supply Construction Manager with enough copies of the Material Safety Data Sheet (MSDS) for the particular material to distribute to all other contractors. Additionally, the Contractor shall provide the Construction Manager with employee safety training procedures for material handling and potential exposure risks.

ARTICLE 11.   RECOURSE BY BUILDER

11.1.   Failure of Performance:

1. <u>Notice to Cure</u>: If Contractor at any time refuses or neglects to supply enough properly skilled workers and proper materials, or fails to properly and diligently prosecute the work covered by this Agreement, or fails to make prompt payment to his workers, subcontractors, or suppliers or becomes delinquent concerning contributions or payments required to be made to any health and welfare, pension, vacation, apprenticeship or other employee benefit program or trust, or is otherwise guilty of a material breach of a provision of this Agreement, and fails within twenty four (24) hours after receipt of notice to commence and continue satisfactory correction of such default with diligence and promptness, then Builder, without prejudice to any right or remedies, shall have the right to any of the following remedies:

   a. supply such number of workers and quantity of materials, equipment and other facilities as Builder deems necessary for the completion of Contractor's work, or any part thereof which Contractor has failed to complete or perform, and charge the cost thereof to Contractor, who shall be liable for the payment of same including reasonable overhead, profit, and actual attorney's fees incurred as a result of Contractor's failure of performance, and

   b. contract with one or more additional Contractors to perform such part of the Contractor's work as the Builder shall determine will provide the most expeditious completion of the total job and charge the cost thereof to the Contractor, and

   c. withhold payment of any monies due Contractor pending corrective action to the extent required by and to the satisfaction of Builder.

In the event of an emergency affecting the safety of persons or property, Builder may proceed as above without notice.

2. <u>Termination for Default</u>: If Contractor fails to commence and satisfactorily continue correction of a default within twenty four (24) hours after receipt by Contractor of the notice issued under Section 11.1 (1)(a), then Builder may terminate Contractor's right to perform under this Agreement and use any materials, implements, equipment, appliances or tools furnished by or belonging to Contractor to complete Contractor's work without further compensation to Contractor for such use. Builder may also provide those materials and equipment, and/or employ such workers or subcontractors as Builder deems necessary to maintain the orderly progress of the work.

    In such a case, Contractor shall be entitled to no further payment until the balance of Contractor's work has been completed. At that time, all of the costs incurred by Builder in performing Contractor's work, including a markup of fifteen percent (15%) for management on such expenses, plus actual attorneys' fees as provided above, shall be deducted from any monies due or to become owing to Contractor. Contractor shall be liable for the payment of any amount by which such expenses may exceed the unpaid balance of the Contract Price.

3. <u>Grounds for withholding Payment</u>: Contractor expressly agrees that payments may be withheld, and all costs incurred by Builder shall be charged against all monies due Contractor under this Agreement or any other Contractor Agreement with Builder if:

    a. Defective work is not remedied; or

    b. Claims of Lien are filed, or reasonable evidence indicates probable filing of claims; or

c. Contractor fails to make prompt and proper payments to his employees, agents, or subcontractors for material, labor, or fringe benefits; or

d. A reasonable doubt by Builder that this Agreement can be completed for the balance then unpaid or under all terms of the contract documents; or

e. Another contractor is damaged by an act for which the Contractor is responsible; or

f. In the opinion of the Builder, the Contractor's work is not progressing satisfactorily; or

g. Penalties are assessed against the Builder or the Contractor for failure of the Contractor to comply with State, Federal, or local laws and regulations; or

h. Any other grounds exist for withholding payment allowed by State or Federal law, or as otherwise provided in this Agreement. When the above matters are rectified, such amounts as then due and owing shall be paid or credited to the Contractor.

ARTICLE 12.   ARBITRATION OF DISPUTES

12.1. Any controversy or claim arising out of or relating to this contract, or the breach thereof, shall be settled by arbitration administered by the American Arbitration Association under its Construction Industry Arbitration Rules in effect at the time of the initiation of the arbitration. Judgment on the award rendered by the arbitrator(s) may be entered in any court having jurisdiction thereof. The result of any such arbitration shall be binding and enforceable in a court of competent jurisdiction. This paragraph shall apply to disputes covered by it even if the Agreement is terminated or rescinded.

ARTICLE 13.   ATTORNEY FEES

13.1. In the event of any arbitration or litigation relating to the project, project performance, or this contract, the prevailing party shall be entitled to reasonable attorney fees, costs, and expenses.

ARTICLE 14.   EXHIBITS

14.1. The following Exhibits are attached hereto and are made a part of this Agreement by this reference thereto:

EXHIBIT "A" – Scope of Work.

EXHIBIT "B" – Contractor's Unit Price Bid Sheet.

EXHIBIT "C" – Specifications.

ARTICLE 15. MISCELLANEOUS

15.1. The Agreement does not give exclusive rights to the Contractor to work with the Builder. The Builder may enter into agreements with other parties in the same trade without affecting the terms of this Agreement.

15.2. The Agreement shall be governed by and interpreted under **(State Name)** law.

15.3. Notices required under the Agreement shall be in writing and delivered to the other party at the address outlined in this Agreement. Such notices may be given in person, by overnight delivery service (prepaid), or by certified mail, return receipt requested. Such notice shall be deemed given when received at such address.

15.4. Each provision of the Agreement is severable from every other provision. If any provision is determined to be unenforceable, the rest of the Agreement shall remain valid and enforceable.

15.5. All plans, drawings, and specifications provided by the Builder to the Contractor shall remain the property of the Builder.

15.6. The term "including" shall mean, including but not limited to, the specific item or matter mentioned.

ARTICLE 16. ENTIRE AGREEMENT

16.1. This Contractor Agreement is solely for the benefit of the signatories hereto and represents the entire and integrated agreement between the parties hereto and supersedes all prior proposals, correspondence, negotiations, or agreements, either written or oral.

ARTICLE 17. ACCEPTANCE

17.1. Certification: Contractor certifies that it: (a) has read the Agreement and understands it; (b) has the skills and qualifications necessary to perform the Work per the Agreement, and to otherwise comply with the Agreement; (c) has all licenses, registrations and similar governmental authorizations necessary to perform the Work and to comply with the Agreement; (d) is familiar with all of the Construction Standards and applicable laws, rules, regulations, codes, documents and other matters mentioned in the Agreement; and (e) has the authority to sign the Agreement. The individual signing on behalf of the Contractor represents and certifies that he is authorized to sign this Agreement on behalf of the Contractor.

WITNESS our hand and seal on this day of _____, 20__.

Signed in the presence of:

_____

Builder's Name   Date

_____

Contractor's Name   Date

One area of the Contractor (Resource) Agreement that provides substantial benefits is *Unit-Based Bid Pricing.* Resource bids that are broken down into pricing for each component of the task allow for obtaining the best possible overall price for the work performed. When multiple bids are presented for the same task by several resources using Unit-Based Bid Pricing, this allows the best price for each component to be negotiated. This type of negotiation ultimately produces two or more resources with the same bid, which also allows for first and second-string resources. When the *Request for Bid* package is presented to the resource (which includes all of the proper documentation the resource needs to present a complete bid), include a Request for Bid cover sheet to outline how the bid is to be submitted. A key statement that must be included in the directions on how to submit a bid is that the bid shall contain each component of the work priced separately, including materials, labor, equipment, profit, and overhead. Additionally, please note that if the bid information is not submitted correctly, the bid will not be accepted or considered. Some resources may be reluctant to submit their bid based on unit pricing because they are hesitant to disclose their unit prices, especially their markup. Inform them that the bid information must be submitted by unit pricing, as without it, neither organization will be operationally excellent and will never reach maximum throughput. Ensure them that their specific bid pricing will never be disclosed or associated with their company's name. Incorporate the longest pricing duration terms into the contract whenever possible. Set the terms to a minimum of a year, without the pricing being adjusted by the resource. In some cases, a period of two years or longer can be achieved. Allow for interim price changes only under specific circumstances. However, the objective here is to maintain budgeted costs for producing the product for a minimum of one year without having to change sales pricing or gross margins.

Be creative. Think outside the box. As another example, a process for material pricing terms was developed with our primary material supplier. This resource had been supplying the bulk of the materials for over twenty years. Trust had been built between both organizations over the years of working together. Lumber, for instance, is a commodity that frequently experiences price fluctuations. To eliminate lumber price fluctuations every thirty to sixty days, both organizations agreed on a new pricing process. Because we had a long history of lumber pricing data, we calculated a five-year running average of lumber prices. Over the past five years, we have observed fluctuations in lumber pricing, ranging from high to low costs. The average high and low prices created our standard deviation points. Both organizations agreed that as long as the current lumber pricing stayed within the standard deviation points, no price adjustments would be made. Over time, the lumber pricing would fluctuate with both price increases

and decreases, where it averaged out that some months one
organization would benefit, and other months the other organization would benefit. But both organizations realized the significant advantages of not having to adjust P.O.s or see gross profits change each time lumber pricing fluctuated. This process was known as Not-to-Exceed *Pricing.*

Other critical areas include accurate material takeoffs and effective supply chain management. After the *Value Engineering and the Unit-Based Bid Pricing* resource contract processes are completed, the purchasing team, in conjunction with each resource that supplies materials, can now complete accurate material takeoffs and lists. Purchase Orders for *Material Packs* can now be broken down and issued, ensuring that only the necessary materials are delivered to the production assembly line with Just-in-Time precision. All the framing lumber used to build an entire house is quite extensive. The *Lumber Pack(s)* delivery tasks and the pertinent P.O.s should be broken down so that all of the framing lumber is not delivered all at once at the beginning of the framing process. Remember, forget about economies of scale; inventory sitting on the ground for days, waiting to be used, is highly inefficient, costly, and unproductive. All materials should be delivered just in time.

Continue to identify every area in the workflow that is open-ended (allowance) and not tied down to specific cost in the budget. A good example in homebuilding is that of site-specific costs. Develop a process within the workflow that determines the exact costs for all items.

Chapter 14

Variances

Now, that I have discussed the importance of having accurate, detailed business plans, budgets, schedules, and production plans, specifications, scopes of work, contracts, and purchase orders I need to talk about *Variances*. As I pointed out earlier, variances are deviations from the anticipated baseline in all these areas. Variances can be both positive and negative, but any variance outside of what was accounted for or expected is costing unnecessary money and is not operational excellence. A great way to start the campaign toward achieving operational excellence is to understand, manage, and eliminate **ALL** variances. Also, find out where the team is *Feeling Pain* in the process and start the improvements there. Review and understand the cause of the variance, then change and enhance the process to eliminate the same future variance.

Many organizations choose to mask their financial variances with contingency dollars instead of tracking the variances and trying to eliminate future unnecessary costs. The same organizations fail to track schedule deviations and are satisfied with what they consider adequate production times. These organizations continue to be less profitable because their thought

process makes them unable or unwilling to invest the time and effort to change and improve. These organizations will never be excellent until they properly address and strive to eliminate all variations, regardless of their type.

How can you manage the multiple variations within your organization? How do you know what to change? It is widely known that 20% of the problems cause 80% of the headaches.

First, there needs to be a process that can identify, quantify, and provide accountability for all variances. Establish *Variance Reason Codes* that cover a wide range of variance types and account for every Variance Purchase Order (V.P.O.) written. The appropriate reason code should be assigned to every V.P.O. as part of the approval process. However, technology and data management alone will not provide you with more control. There must be processes firmly in place that are engineered or improved that work toward eliminating the same future variance. Effectively manage every identified variance throughout the entire organization, especially in the areas described below.

1. **Business Plan** - (Sales, Starts, and Closings) Minimize costly finished goods inventory.

2. **Financial** - Create a budget that is as realistic as possible. Work toward minimizing or eliminating contingencies and allowances.
3. **Schedule** - Produce your product as quickly and efficiently as possible. This will enable you to sell and close soon; the customer has a short timeline requirement.
4. **Documentation** - continue to strive for defect-free documentation in all areas.
5. **Process** - Ongoing improvement and enhancement of each process with every identified variance.

Research and Development (R&D) is a crucial function for every area of the organization and should be ongoing at all times. Not just the product, but all processes as well. R&D the product before production begins to establish expected baselines and to minimize variances. Produce prototypes whenever possible. Keep in mind that situations or tasks are constantly changing, creating some variance.

I want to provide a real-life example of the incredibly positive financial impact one organization achieved by following a process to eliminate all variances. Upon my arrival, the organization was struggling to manage its variances in all areas. Although a P.O. and V.P.O. system was in place, it was far from being used effectively. This homebuilding organization was averaging forty-five

V.P.O.s per new home built, with an average of $ 35,000 in unbudgeted costs per house. Thus, with an average selling price of $350,000.00 per home, they were experiencing a 10% cost overrun. At that time, the

organization was producing approximately 500 new homes annually. At an unbudgeted cost per home of $35,000.00, multiplied by 500 homes per year, there was an unexpected cost overrun of over $ 17 million annually.

A massive margin erosion, again and again. Not to mention the additional costs incurred to manage and execute all those VPOs. We estimated that each V.P.O. that had to be written had an associated combined administration cost of at least $75.00, and that was conservative. With 45 V.P.O.s being written per house, at $75.00 each, and 500 houses per year, this equaled an additional unnecessary expense of almost $2 million. *All variances, regardless of the type, are costly*. The annual variance costs totaled over **$19 million** per year. The variance of the expenses alone was over 9% of the total annual sales revenue. We needed to stop the bleeding, and we needed to do it rapidly.

One of the first initiatives we implemented was the requirement that every V.P.O. had a *Variance Reason Code* (VRC) associated with it. We created every VRC we thought was appropriate and added new ones as needed. We had some historical variance reasons, but the data was vague and not always sufficient or accurate. Virtually every function of the organization was producing V.P.O.s. As I stated earlier, we embarked on a journey of ongoing process improvement to eliminate all variances. With a drastic improvement in the data variance, we began to quickly identify which functions and processes were producing the most variance and which required the most attention. Always attack the *low-hanging fruit* first. Quick successes bred more success. Most of the deficiencies and variances were discovered and brought to light by the Production Managers (PMs) once production began. They were quick to identify the origin of the defect because they were held accountable for the quality and timely completion of each production task. With the Production Managers also being held responsible for overall schedule compliance, it became evident that they needed to be an integral part of managing the timely correction of any discovered defect, regardless of the origin, once the product had started on the assembly line. We required quick and accurate communication, along with resolution of all variances, to ensure the correct reason code was communicated. This allowed us to correct the appropriate process and prevent the same type of variance from being repeated. We instituted that, once a variance was discovered during production, the Production Manager was jointly responsible for the accurate and timely resolution of the defect, regardless of its origin. We termed it *"Throw the rock **back** over the wall with a string tied to it"*. Throughout the entire organization, hold the upline function accountable for their defects by pulling the cord and sending the defective work back for correction. Hold them accountable by having them agree to a time when the corrected work will be returned. For example, the PM would communicate with the variance origin function and negotiate an agreement on when the corrected defect could be expected to be returned, allowing production to resume if the PM did not receive the corrected defect on or before the agreed upon time the PM was required to call (*Tug on the string*) to check on the status of the correction and to hold the function accountable to the agreement. Holding the PM responsible for each variance they identified assured that every defect was quickly communicated and thus eliminated. The objective was that the entire organization was responsible for *Quality Control* and that every identified defect was eliminated. Quality will increase with every process improvement.

 After one of the Monthly Production Managers' Meetings, a Regional PM, along with a PM, approached me to complain that it was unfair that they were being held responsible for variances and VPOs that originated in another department or function. I said to them, "I want you both to be completely honest with me. Would you even be talking about variances and V.P.O.s with me now if you were not held accountable to help manage them"? They both answered, "Probably not." I replied, "I rest my case". They now fully understood the objective. Everyone associated with the organization must know that they are equally responsible for communicating, learning from, managing, and eliminating variances and VPOs.

Defects or variances of any type that impact constrained tasks should always take top priority. Teach every member of the organization that if a defect is discovered during a constrained activity, they should immediately stop what they are doing and take whatever necessary steps to correct the defect, thereby minimizing delay time as rapidly as possible. Remember, time lost on a constraint is time lost forever. Something will need to be adjusted to make the time up, if even possible, and it **WILL ALWAYS** be costly. If the result is a delayed throughput, it can be **expensive**. Keeping accurate schedule variance data, such as start dates and completion dates on a constrained task, is also vitally important.

Chapter 15

Produce EXCELLENT Products and Services

Excellent quality products and services, along with their ongoing improvement, are the responsibility of everyone associated with your organization, including subcontractors, suppliers, consultants, lenders, and customers. Producing excellent products and services can effectively differentiate the organization from its competitors. Always focus on product and service excellence as you improve your processes. It is not enough to produce a quality product and/or service. Ongoing improvement in every area should always be pursued, especially in terms of continuing profitability improvement. Every product improvement is productive and will help the organization achieve its goal of generating revenue.

The production of a quality product requires the implementation and proper execution of a combination of several key philosophies. Total Quality Management (TQM), Six Sigma, Lean Manufacturing, and the Theory of Constraints (T.O.C.) all possess necessary methodologies that are highly critical to producing a quality, efficient, and profitable product or service.

Let us discuss the topic of *Quality Control Inspections*. Quality control inspections should be limited throughout The workflow system is implemented only in areas where it is most productive. However, suppose your team is not accustomed to these principles and consistently producing high-quality work throughout the system. In that case, you must randomly *inspect what you expect* for a time until they learn and become proficient. Quality Control Inspections should be done ahead of any constrained task. Lost time due to Quality Control Inspections or defects found in activities after going through the constraint results in lost throughput. Remember, the example is based on just one day of lost throughput. It can and usually does equate to **a tremendous amount of money lost**.

Every function and task within the organization should be held to *Zero Defects* quality standards. They must fully understand that NO WORK is to be allowed to move down line to another work center with a known defect. Picture the automobile assembly line. Everyone has seen this, either on television or perhaps in person. Imagine that your task on the assembly line is to install the four doors on the car. The task above you is to install the door hinges so the doors can be installed. Let's assume that, because of a defect, the up-line work center was only able to get three of the required four hinges installed on the car. They are necessary to *pull the Chord* to stop the assembly line to address the problem. The assembly line is stopped; a red light begins flashing over the work center that pulled the chord, so everyone knows where the problem has occurred. You can no longer work on the following product because the assembly line has been stopped. You join in to help correct the defect because everyone on the line has been taught that they are equally responsible for remedying any known defect. If, for some reason, the car is allowed to move down the line to your work center with only three door hinges, you must pull the cord once the defect is discovered. Each known defect must be addressed and corrected immediately. Once the defect is corrected, the assembly line is restarted.

Inspection of quality and completion is already a part of some job descriptions' daily critical few. If necessary, establish regular quality inspection points throughout the workflow system. After discipline to quality standards has been established, random quality control inspections should be required only occasionally. Also, always make sure every task is fully completed and ready for the next task. **On an assembly line, if you do not think you have the time to fix the defect right away, how will you find the time to fix it later?** To make the above statement easier to comprehend, imagine an assembly line running continuously, twenty-four hours a day, seven days a week. The product with the discovered defect cannot simply be pulled off the assembly line to be addressed at a later time. There is no last time in this example. Plus, the discovered defect loses the sense of urgency for immediate correction if it is allowed to be addressed later. Always consider *TIME* a precious commodity. Time truly equates to money. Like money, time should never be wasted. **The objective is to continually produce a high-quality product as fast and efficiently as possible**. If the organization accomplishes this, it WILL achieve ongoing profitability.

I firmly believe that the individuals who say speed sacrifices quality have misguided thinking. If the correct processes are in place, ongoing improvements are being made, operational excellence is the mindset of the entire organization, and speed is achieved throughout the whole workflow system, then outstanding products will be produced quickly and ever-increasing profits will be realized.

Strive to continually produce what I refer to as *"Bullet Proof Products"*. What I mean by 'bulletproof' is to create such a high quality that no one can complain about (or find flaws in) the product or service. By setting the proper quality expectations with both the customer and the organization, and by adhering to strict quality standards without exception, an excellent product will be delivered. One way to ensure excellent products is to develop a process where the completed product is accepted by the function responsible for warranting the product before it is delivered to the customer. The warranty function conducts a final quality inspection to ensure that the product meets the expected quality standards. If any defect is discovered, it is corrected right away. Once the product passes the final quality inspection, it is accepted and turned over to warranty for management of the warranty process. Some homebuilders have the Production Manager responsible for their warranty. Whatever the case, a final quality inspection is necessary to hold the production function accountable and ensure it achieves the required quality standard. In homebuilding, this quality inspection should occur before the customer is shown the finished product during the *New Home Orientation*. The New Home Orientation is a prescheduled event during which the home is presented to the customer to explain the systems, maintenance, and warrantable items that may arise in the future. This should not be considered an opportunity for the customer to inspect the product. All quality standards have been met. At this event, the customer accepts the product as complete. Additionally, in homebuilding, as part of the warranty process, routine post-delivery visits to the product are necessary to ensure proper quality is maintained. Typically, there are two visits, which are conducted ninety days and one year after delivery of the product. Each visit is preplanned to address specific warranty-covered issues. However, the expectation should be communicated to the customer that any warrantable issue will be addressed immediately. The objective here is to be completely proud of the product that is delivered. It is extremely necessary to have a strong warranty process in place that is executed with precision and excellence.

Always stand behind the product and service that is delivered. Focus on continually improving the quality of product delivery and warranty processes. By doing so, you will reap the benefits of being an excellent organization that consistently prioritizes the customer's needs.

Chapter 16

Ongoing Improvement, Never Give Up

The journey to operational excellence will undoubtedly become stormy and controversial. It will get challenging at times. The team may become discouraged and wonder if all the changes are worth it. Remember, nothing worth achieving is ever easy. It takes a **team** that has determination and a strong will to continue improving until the best is achieved and maintained. Additionally, it requires a strong leader who, when knocked down, quickly gets back up, dusts themselves off, and keeps moving forward. They have a positive, *never-say-never* attitude. Continue the journey of engineering excellent processes and systems all the time, in every task of your business. Even when the organization is operationally excellent, keep focused on and strive for improvement. Jack Welch, the former CEO of General Electric, once said, "If the rate of change outside of your organization is greater than the rate of change within, you are moving backwards and dying".

REAP THE BENEFITS OF OPERATIONAL EXCELLENCE

Focus on achieving the daily details and requirements of each process. If you do this every day, then the weekly
and monthly process requirements will be met. I have the mantra: **"Operations with Excellence Every Day"**.

God says in Psalm 112, "You can do all things through Christ who gives us strength". We need to have faith. Trust and believe that *ALL* of God's words and promises are true. If we genuinely believe that God loves us, that He gives us unending grace sufficient for every situation, that He provides mercy when we make mistakes, then we can live in His peace, knowing that He will give us wisdom when we ask Him and direct our steps. It is such a remarkable thing that Jesus did for each one of us. Because He died and rose again to completely pay for our sins, if we repent of our sins, and we believe that Jesus is our only Lord and Savior, then we can all trust that we will spend eternity with Him.

We have to have faith in what God has given us and the things we know. Do not be reluctant to move forward. Take one step at a time. Complete each step with excellence. Do not take shortcuts. Never compromise on what you know to be right. At times, there may be immense pressure to compromise your principles, but if you stand true to God's teachings, He promises to bless you beyond what you can imagine. If you do compromise, there is a tremendous price to pay—comment on doing everything with excellence. Keep working your faith. **NEVER GIVE UP and NEVER GIVE IN.**

Psalm 127: "Unless the Lord builds the house, its builder's labor is in vain".

www.ingramcontent.com/pod-product-compliance
Lightning Source LLC
Chambersburg PA
CBHW070245190526
45169CB00001B/313